LIVERPOOL
MEMORIES

The publishers would like to thank the following companies for their

support in the production of this book

Main Sponsor
Jaguar

Beesley & Fildes Limited

Blue Coat School, Liverpool

Walter Craven

Dompak Grosvenor

Everton Glassworks

FWL Technologies Limited

GlaxoSmithKline

Liverpool Housing Trust

Liver Housing Association (now called Arena Housing Association)

Thomas Loughlin Limited

AF & D Mackay

R L Martindale Limited

John Mason International Limited

Mersey Cabs Limited

Mersey Towel Service (Laundry) Limited

William Rainford (Holdings) Limited

Rea Metal Windows Limited

Robinson Willey

Roystons

The Venmore Partnership

Wrenco (Contractors) Limited

First published in Great Britain by True North Books Limited
England HX3 6AE
01422 344344

ISBN 1 903204 53 4

Text, design and origination by True North Books Limited
Printed and bound by The Amadeus Press Limited

LIVERPOOL
MEMORIES

Contents

Page 8
Around the city's streets

Page 26
Events & occasions

Page 46
At leisure

Page 54
Wartime

Page 58
Bird's eye view

Page 66
On the move

Page 72
Shopping spree

Page 84
Making a living

Introduction

Do you remember those sweets that we used to call 'Gob-stoppers'? Sometimes they were known as 'bulls eyes'. They had several hard layers, but each layer was sweet and different from the last. They changed colour as each lining dissolved in the mouth to reveal the next colour. Once the centre was reached, it was soft and even sweeter. Liverpool's a bit like that. It has several different layers and a soft heart. It's what gives the people their apparently unique character?

A considerable amount of talent has burst forth from the city over the years. This book is not big enough to enter all of the famous show business names, but they have introduced their hometown of Liverpool to the world. People in America may never have visited Penny Lane, but they certainly are aware of its existence. Children everywhere know who mines what at Knotty Ash, and they can even sing songs about them. Add any well known footballers from Liverpool or Everton, and any historical characters who have had an influence on all our lives, and the roll of Liverpool fame is almost endless. Tourists travel from all corners of the world to gaze in wonder at the Cavern nightclub, where the Beatles performed on stage. The alley has now become a shrine for ardent fans. They visit the museum at the Albert Dock that tells the Beatles Story. Beatles pilgrims climb aboard minibuses for trips to number 20 Forthlin Road, the former home of the McCartney family, where Paul and John Lennon met and wrote several of their early songs.

Even MPs from this city are, apparently, like no others. At the funeral of Bessie Braddock, who was known and admired by people from outside Liverpool as well as within, Harold Wilson said that she could only be fully understood in the context of Liverpool. She was a product of her city and of her generation.

Liverpool owes its early existence to King John. He wanted a port, from which he could ship his soldiers and goods too and from Ireland, which was fairly free from attack by

Children enjoying a train ride at English Electric's Show in the 1940s.

the Welsh. There was a sort of castle there already. It stood on a hill in the vicinity of Derby Square and Castle Street. King John may have found a use for it, for it would then have been a gentle sloping hill overlooking the estuary.

The first wet dock was created in the Mersey, although it is reported that it had a tendency to silt up. Over the years its importance as a port grew. The increasing trade with the West Indies brought wealth in the form of 'sugar and spice, and all things nice', as the nursery rhyme would have us believe, but this was not entirely the case. Most things were good, like cotton, sugar, spice and tobacco, but there also were fortunes made from the trade in slaves. Pirates sailed from the Mersey to raid the Spanish ships. The Spanish may have considered them to be 'pirates', but at home they were 'business men', and 'patriots'.

Liverpool became linked with Manchester by the canal and by rail. George Stephenson was commissioned to build a railway. At the same time a Yorkshire-man called Jesse Hartley was doing great things in the town. He improved the docks building in his favourite material - granite. So well were they built that they withstood the punishment of German bombs in 1941. Sailors from all parts of the globe know the approach to Liverpool docks, which once challenged London for the title of the biggest and busiest. It was the first that many American soldiers saw of 'the old country' when they landed in England before moving on to fight in Europe. The Yanks experienced the warmth and generosity of the people as they were, unceremoniously, dumped on the people who had no choice in having them, but welcomed them warmly nevertheless. Brave merchant seamen, sailing from the port, kept the country supplied with vital goods at great risk to their own lives. The Western Approaches Command, stationed in Derby House, planned and won the Battle of the Atlantic.

Great ships have been built and launched from the shipyards of the Mersey. In the days of the clipper ships, the tall ships were a familiar sight in the estuary. Those that still exist regularly visit, and regard this as an essential stop on their tours.

In the early 1900s Cunard and White Star ships provided luxury travel across the Atlantic. It must have been an incredible sight to see thousands of people lining the banks of the river to watch the Lusitania leave on her maiden voyage to New York. The four-funnelled ship made the crossing in a record time of four days, nine hours and fifty-two minutes. Later the Mauritania improved on this time. Many families lost loved ones when the Titanic sank. Even though she did not sail from

Liverpool Libraries and Information Services

Dodging the traffic in Church Street in 1947.

Liverpool there were many crewmen on board who were Liverpudlians. The same was also true when a German submarine sank the Lusitania in 1915. It was thought to be a cowardly way to wage a war. One thousand three hundred lives were lost. Many of them were women and children.

The longest ship to sail into the Mersey was 'The British Argosy' in the 60s. She was probably the heaviest too at one hundred and seven thousand seven hundred and twenty-nine tons. Many great ships have been built and launched in the Mersey. Cammel Laird shipyard closed in April 1992 after 165 years of shipbuilding. Memories of this maritime heritage have been lovingly preserved in, and around, the Albert Dock.

The railway brought many passengers to the docks, some who were wealthy and famous, and some who were poor. In a manner of speaking, the railway itself was transported to America. The 'Flying Scotsman' was hoisted aboard a ship in 1969, and sailed across to Boston. One hundred and sixty tons in weight and sixty feet long, it had retired from service in 1963. This, the first train to break the one hundred mile per hour speed limit, is now back in Britain fully restored. The port has seen double-decker buses leave for America! A consignment of Leyland buses was transported to New York for 'London Bus Week'. (Before anyone asks, there has been no mistake, 'London Bus Week' was held in New York, not London, in 1952!)

A walk around the city reveals much. It is only a short distance across Stanley Park from the Kop at Anfield to the Everton ground of Goodison Park, but any supporter will tell you that it is a million miles.

A stroll around the centre reveals architectural gems the equal of any in the country. Bluecoat Chambers, built shortly after the reign of Queen Anne, provides a home for the Arts and is a fine example of its style. There are narrow shopping alleys to contrast with the grand scale of the classical St George's Hall. The functional arched roof of the railway station, and the practical Beacon tower, the controversial frame-ribbed Metropolitan Cathedral and the Liverpool Cathedral, which is the largest Anglican Church in the world, all demonstrate the variety, ingenuity, artistry and spirituality of the people of Liverpool.

Turn the pages of this book and sample a little of the atmosphere of a living and vibrant, ever changing City. Enjoy, and possibly regret, the things that have been lost, but balance that with the changes, many of which have been good for the citizens of Liverpool.

Not a vehicle is moving on this day in July 1947. It is Tuesday and Broadbridges are doing good business. The National Health Service was established in the previous year and spectacles and dentures were 'free'. Of course everyone was making a contribution to the system, but in only four years time the government would be forced to introduce charges for glasses and dentures. Many people were obtaining them simply because they were available. It almost became fashionable to do so. 'Fashionable' is, perhaps, not the word that the children, who had to wear National Health glasses at school, would have used to describe them. They were wire rimmed, plastic covered, unimaginative circles covering the eyes. They were held in place by spring hooks over the ears. They were practical, cheap, but far from flattering. There was little to be found in the shops. Meat, poultry and eggs, were almost luxury items. The wheat crop had been poor this year after an extremely severe winter. Bread had been rationed in the previous year, which was something that had not happened even during the war. Grain from Europe was being diverted to Germany, where a state of famine existed. The government had recommended that people go out and catch squirrels to make squirrel pie - and they were serious! There was some good news to cheer the people in 1947. The marriage of Princess Elizabeth to Prince Philip of Greece took place. Even she had to get extra coupons to obtain the material for her wedding dress because material was still rationed.

Around the city's streets

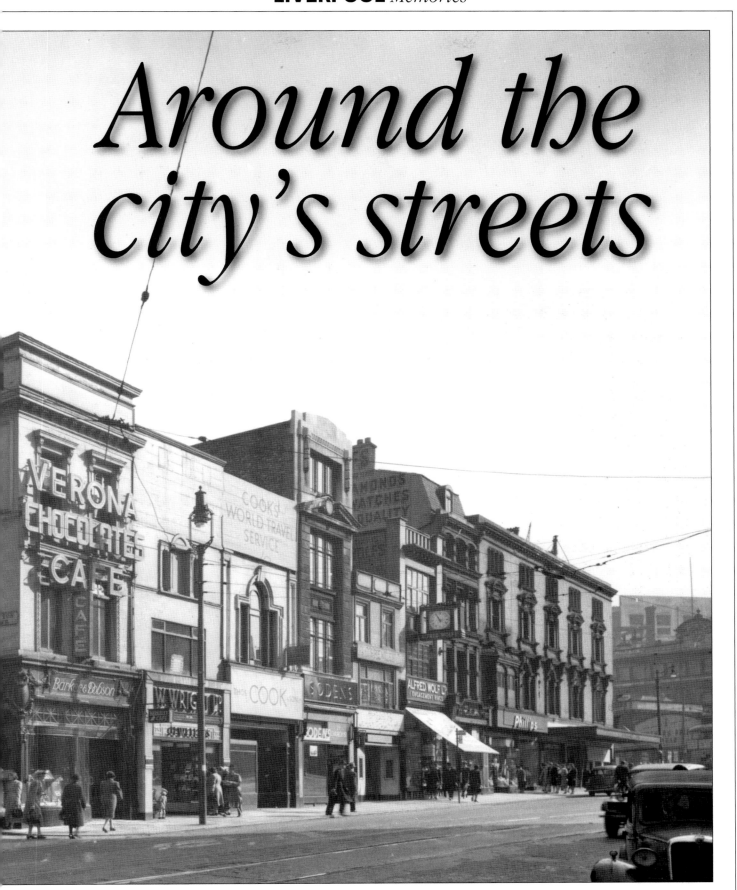

Above: There is no fear that the air raid warning will sound for the war is over. It was 1948 when the damage to these buildings, which was caused by a bomb, was recorded on film. In 2002 the corner of Hanover Street and College Lane is still empty and awaiting development. As the young ladies chat on their way to work they may be talking about the nationalisation of the railways, which has taken place this month, or the proposed nationalisation of the electricity industry. In only a few short months the National Health Act of 1946 would be implemented and it would be possible to get a free prescription for spectacles or dentures. They may be grumbling about the shortages of material, and their continued 'make do and mend', or about the difficulty in buying even a simple thing like a zip fastener. Since the factories that used to make them had been turned to the manufacture of armaments, they were only now returning to 'normal service'. By the end of the year they will have good news to debate when Princess Elizabeth gives birth to a son, Charles Phillip Arthur George. Running parallel with College Lane, on the extreme right of the picture, is School Street. Between the two lies an architectural gem by any standards, which was luckily missed by the bombs. The 'Bluecoat', Bluecoat Chambers, was originally built as a school. It has since been home to many others including the Sandon Studios Society, a group of artists and musicians.

Elliot Street has changed greatly since the forties. The cobbled streets, which were so familiar then, are now a rare sight. They have somehow achieved the status of the 'picturesque'. The trams and their overhead wires have rolled into the history books. Simpson's Boot and Shoe shop, the 'Villiers' public house, the premises of John Pride & Sons ladies hairdressers, Harold Davies licensed victualler and Jackson's boot and shoe shop have all been replaced by the modern shopping centre. If we take a closer look at the top of the street, just above the tram we can see the Forum cinema. The Crown Hotel is visible on the extreme left. The Crown, the Forum, and the block next to the cinema, have all survived the changes of time. How much we looked forward to our Saturday morning, or afternoon, visits to the cinema in the days before television and Bingo took over. It could be as little as four pence to sit on the first two rows. How we shouted when the film broke. 'Put a penny in the meter!' was one of the more polite comments. When the film resumed it was greeted with the loudest cheer. Those were the days when you knew that the 'baddy' was the one in the black outfit. The hero always wore white and rode into the sunset on a white horse. Before television put paid to the pictures and the radio, we would eagerly gather around the wireless and listen for the familiar music, which heralded the start of another adventure of Dick Barton and his chum 'Snowy' White. We were desperate to discover how they had escaped the impossible situation we had left him in during the last episode. He always escaped and gave the villain his just deserts.

Oakfield Road looked a little different in 1948. Its cobble surface was inset with tramlines polished to a shine by iron wheels. They caused much trouble for cyclists. Care had to be taken to cross them at an angle, by cars as well as cyclists and motorcyclists. If they were not treated with that respect they would take charge of the steering and deposit the rider into the road, or pull the unwary driver along until control was restored. The cobbles became polished, and, with a thin coating of rubber, oil, and rain, soon became slippery and dangerous.

The tramlines, like the canals and rivers, shone in the moonlight and were very visible from the air. During the war such a moon was called a 'bomber's moon, as it clearly guided them to their targets.

The first Supermarket has opened in London. But customers, who patronised the shops in Oakfield Road in 1948, would have found the idea of taking things from a shelf and placing them into a basket strange and a little like stealing. They preferred to be served by someone they knew. They waited patiently in line, for the war had taught them to queue and wait their turn, until the familiar question, 'Who is next?' was asked. If there was one aspect of good manners that became so engrained in the British it was to politely wait their turn. They would form an orderly queue even if they were alone!

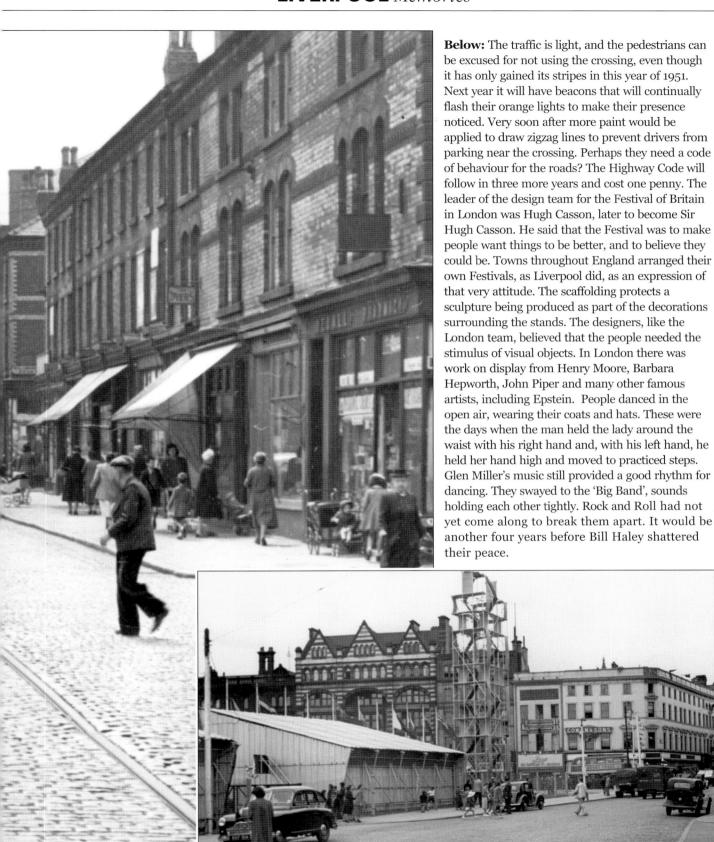

Below: The traffic is light, and the pedestrians can be excused for not using the crossing, even though it has only gained its stripes in this year of 1951. Next year it will have beacons that will continually flash their orange lights to make their presence noticed. Very soon after more paint would be applied to draw zigzag lines to prevent drivers from parking near the crossing. Perhaps they need a code of behaviour for the roads? The Highway Code will follow in three more years and cost one penny. The leader of the design team for the Festival of Britain in London was Hugh Casson, later to become Sir Hugh Casson. He said that the Festival was to make people want things to be better, and to believe they could be. Towns throughout England arranged their own Festivals, as Liverpool did, as an expression of that very attitude. The scaffolding protects a sculpture being produced as part of the decorations surrounding the stands. The designers, like the London team, believed that the people needed the stimulus of visual objects. In London there was work on display from Henry Moore, Barbara Hepworth, John Piper and many other famous artists, including Epstein. People danced in the open air, wearing their coats and hats. These were the days when the man held the lady around the waist with his right hand and, with his left hand, he held her hand high and moved to practiced steps. Glen Miller's music still provided a good rhythm for dancing. They swayed to the 'Big Band', sounds holding each other tightly. Rock and Roll had not yet come along to break them apart. It would be another four years before Bill Haley shattered their peace.

Below: Bunney's has disappeared from this junction, as did many buildings in this area when enemy bombers blitzed the city. In Bunney's case, it was the developer's bulldozer that did its work. Barratt's now occupy the site. Cooper's Buildings, on the extreme right survived. Now, on the opposite corner, where Hope Brothers once traded, there is a 'Gap'. Not a space, nor a 'jowler' or a 'jigger', but a modern shop. Quite what the people would have made of such a name for a shop, before the war, can only be guessed.

The trams have long rolled away and cars, vans and lorries take second place to the pedestrians. The road surface is easier on the ankles than the uneven cobbles and tram tracks used to be.

Such saloon cars as these parked in Paradise Street could be provided in any colour, just so long as it was black. It had much to do with the technology of paint. Any other colour was difficult to produce which was resistant to the heat of the bonnet above the engine, or resistant to cracking as the body flexed with the vibration of the moving car, despite being built on a rigid chassis. How 'modern' the mono-cocque bodied cars of the fifties seemed when they were first produced. They could then be made in other colours, and be fitted with white wall tyres, and lots of chrome fittings. They reflected the freedom and increasing affluence of their time. But here, in the forties, the simple, black, modest cars, capable of returning more miles to the gallon, are more suited to their day when the effects of war were ever present.

Liverpool Libraries and Information Services

I t must be the late 1940s when the policeman kept the traffic flowing smoothly at the junction of London Road and Commutation Row. Sadly they were eventually replaced by traffic lights. 'Robos', as the robotic lights were named, were not as interesting to watch as the policemen. Some would wave with great vigour, as if to be telling the drivers to get away quick, others would adopt a more nonchalant style of apparent indifference. They raised a hand to stop the traffic, and revelled in the power. Trams must have been given priority, because their brakes were not quite as efficient as those of a car, and the brakes of a car were not so wonderful on the slippery surface of a cobbled road. Some junctions had striped boxes for the traffic bobby to stand in and be noticed. On this junction he has only a tiny circular area beneath a lamppost to stand on whilst performing his duty. A gesture has been made to bring his presence to the notice of drivers. For his protection the base of the lamppost has been painted with black and white stripes.

Montague Burton's once provided a full range of gentlemen's suits, from the reasonably priced, affordable with the coupon issued to every ex-serviceman as he was demobbed (demobilised) from the army, to the best, worsted cloths for the discerning gentleman. The soldier would get a jacket, waistcoat and trousers, from 'Monty's', in fact it was 'the full Monty'. This is a slightly different meaning from the present day use of the expression.

Below: Williamson Square is a car enthusiast's dream. In 1946 there may have been less choice of colour, but there seemed to be a greater variety, or is that just because we look back through rose-coloured spectacles? They had to be started with care on a cold morning. The choke had to be pulled just the right amount to allow sufficient petrol without causing it to flood. The engine had to have achieved the right temperature before the choke could be released or the engine stalled at the junction. The skill of double-de-clutching is almost a lost art. For those not familiar with the early gearboxes, in order to change gear the engine revolutions had to be right before the gears would engage smoothly. This meant that the clutch was depressed twice in any change

Liverpool Libraries and Information Services

of gear. It's fun trying to name the car. Can anyone see a Riley, or an Austin Ruby? What about that great name in motoring, the Wolseley? Across the Square is the Playhouse. Many a famous artist has 'trod the boards' at the Playhouse. Rex Harrison, who was born in Liverpool was told, that acting was not really for him, and 'had he thought of anything else?' Other household names have performed in this theatre. Derek Nimmo was on stage here long before he 'beamed up' to the Enterprise, and John Gregson, before he owned a car called 'Genevieve', Brian Reece and Deryck Guyler, to name but a very few.

On the right of the picture is Dix Brothers, trimming manufacturers, and far right, on the corner of Basnett Street are the premises of George Henry Lee, fashion specialists.

Bottom: These superb buildings luckily survived the air raids. In July 1948, when this picture was taken, the shelters were still in place at Pier Head. Strong gates now block the doorways, but during the war the paths to them had to be clear and free. When the siren wailed the warning of approaching enemy aircraft, everyone ran to the nearest shelter, hurried along by the Air Raid Warden. Some people's homes had reinforced cellars, or they had corrugated iron Anderson shelters in their gardens. Buried deep and covered with earth, such shelters afforded reasonable protection until the siren sounded the 'All Clear'.

For those who did not have a garden, the Morrison shelter was the alternative. It was a steel cage, which when not in use, could double as a table and be covered with a cloth. It was strong enough to survive the collapse of the building around it, but it must have been a nightmare for any trapped victim waiting to be rescued. Some such shelters survived in parks and school playgrounds well into the fifties. Many a naughty boy has taken a candle and a box of matches from the stock kept in the pantry in case of a power cut. With his spoils concealed under the Fair Isle jersey, which Granny had knitted using bits of spare wool, he sneaked down to the shelter to meet his friends. It was fun huddling around the candle telling frightening stories. Many an older boy has used the darkness of the shelter to hide himself, and the girl he was courting, from public view. These were educational establishments!

Below: Major reconstruction was underway at the junction of Lord Street and Church Street on this busy shopping day in 1955. Having lived through the years of austerity all rationing had gone, for many it was still only 'window-shopping' at British Home Stores, Hope Brothers and the rest.

Those few, who were wealthy enough to have owned a television set in 1952 in time for the coronation, would now be out buying one capable of broadcasting the second, new, commercial programme. To combat the first broadcast of this independent channel on 22nd September 1955, the BBC took a drastic and severe step. In the ever-popular soap opera 'The Archers', they decided to have Grace Archer burned to death in a fire. However, it would have been impossible to plan such an event every night, and Independent Television was here to stay. The first product ever to be advertised on television was Gibbs SR Toothpaste. Maybe some readers will remember what SR stood for.

These were the days when ladies and gentlemen dressed 'properly' when they went to town. Hat, tailored overcoat, and tie were the order of the day for the men. There is no evidence of the new phenomenon, 'teenagers', on this day in Church Street. Perhaps they were out buying there 'Teddy' suits so that they could look their best when they rioted in the cinema as Bill Haley and the Comets 'Rocked Around The Clock'.

The trams would, within two short years, vanish from the streets of Liverpool, but the Minor Thousand, would become the best selling car ever in four short years.

Right: The flags also flew above Dale Street in 1951. What a good view of the traffic and pedestrians from the top of the Town Hall. It was possible to climb aboard a tram, and, for a few pence, travel down to Pier Head. The pennies were those coppers, some of which we called 'bun' pennies, because the young Victoria had her hair tied in a bun at the back of her head. Coins were bigger and heavier and could be jingled in the pocket. The old half-crown was a heavy silver coin bearing a royal shield and worth two shillings and six pence. Do you remember the twelve sided three-penny piece?

Down the road a mist is forming. Hopefully it is a sea fret, or just a morning mist, and not one of those 'smogs' that were causing problems. Smoke combined with fog to form a thick, sooty, almost impenetrable blanket over the towns. The year after this picture was taken, London was stricken with the worst smog it had ever experienced. From 1953 it was possible to obtain smog masks through the NHS. During that time thousands of Londoners died of heart or lung diseases. The Clean Air Act was passed four years later and it allowed local authorities to create smokeless zones. The Act came into full force in 1958.

It is becoming clear that, with the rapid increase in the number of cars on the roads, the days of the tram were numbered. The tram cannot manoeuvre around parked vehicles, nor can it take evasive action to avoid the car pulling away from the kerb.

Liverpool Libraries and Information Services

Liverpool Libraries and Information Services

Left: Late evening shoppers take advantage of the last few hours to pick up bargains at St John's market in 1962. Sunblinds, at almost all of the shops down the length of Elliot Street, protect the goods in the windows. Radical changes in our shopping methods were occurring. It was not unusual to find a notice in the shop window saying, 'Closed for alterations'. When a shop did eventually reopen, the marble topped counters had disappeared and when the only assistant to be seen was asked for a tin of treacle, the unfamiliar response was, 'Second shelf down the first aisle'. We didn't like to take things from the shelves. It was almost like stealing. There were no longer paper bags hanging from a string. The bacon slicer had vanished. The biscuit tins had been replaced with packets. The wooden floors were now covered. There was less of the usual chitchat as we waited at the till in this new 'self-service' shop. It was quicker, but this new idea, like TV, would only be a temporary fashion, we thought, it will never catch-on. Once the old market was demolished, we were not sure if the replacement would be better or worse. It is certainly a different shopping experience. The new complex is bright, warm, and pleasant. There are still a few cars, travelling along the one-way street, with running boards and wing mudguards. Like the old market, they too will eventually succumb to progress.

Below: Seeming to have all the cares of the world on her shoulders this attractive young woman crossed the Strand by the Goree in 1961. A penny for her thoughts might bring a pound's worth of information. Could she have harked back to the times when her grandpa took her on the overhead railway for a treat so that she could get a first class view of the sights of the city? Perhaps her mind was focused upon something more recent. Had she been stood up by some ungracious beau, condemning her to a lonely evening in front of the TV watching 'Emergency Ward 10'? As she trudged across the setts it might have been something as simple as a problem at the office that occupied her mind. Whatever it was, it had her full attention. Our subject of conjecture was obviously a modern miss, with her mid calf skirt, neat blouse and stylish short hair. Not for her the hat or headscarf that older or less fashionable women sported, for she went bareheaded as though to say that she was not hiding her talents underneath a millinery bushel. In a few short years she would be at the forefront of women's liberation as she stated her case for equality. In the meantime we can only ponder the cause of the trouble that made such a pretty pair of shoulders droop so forlornly.

Above: Looking down on the market from Blackler's roof, Great Charlotte Street is busy in about 1961. In two short years the demolition experts will be at work in the area, but for now it is business as usual. Everyone quietly going about their business, and not a single one of Walt Disney's 'One Hundred and One Dalmatians' to be seen anywhere. No sign of any soldiers either as there is peace and prosperity and national service is at an end. The King tried to avoid national service in America, but eventually had to step into uniform in 1960, even if only for a short time. 'The King', of course, was Elvis Presley. Tension may be high between East and West, and the 'iron curtain', which Churchill spoke about, had descended, but the greatest threat to society, according to the newspapers of the time, was the printing of an unexpurgated version of 'Lady Chatterley's Lover', by D H Lawrence. Perhaps it is possible to get a copy from the market? It is still possible to buy a good tin bath at the market, and a good thing too. Whilst the majority of homes now had an inside toilet, and grants available to fit a bathroom aswell, some still had to fill the tin bath in front of the fire. This gave the music hall comedians continued material for stories. The old boiler, mangle and scrubbing board were steadily being replaced by electric, twin-tub washing machines. An improvement though they were, they still needed to be alongside the sink in order to be filled with water via a rubber pipe connected to the tap. Having washed the clothes in one of the tubs, they were transferred, using hand held wooden pincers; to the spinner to receive a rinse and a final spin dry.

Motoring enthusiasts and nostalgia buffs will love reminiscing about the names of the manufacturers and models on view in this 1957 scene as the camera looks towards the overhead railway. Austin, Singer, Morris, Ford, Standard, Sunbeam and Wolseley are just some of those on view, with Popular, Prefect, Traveller, Minor and Vanguard acting as other names for us to conjure with. Try to find a Datsun, Honda, Nissan, Toyota or Subaru and you are in for a lengthy search. Even Renault and Volkswagen would be hard to find on a British car park in those days. There was something quaintly touching about the names of the cars we had when motoring was still a joy and the motorway, multi storey car park and traffic warden were yet to make their mark. Riley Elf and Hillman Imp have a special sparkle and ring to the ears that no Peugeot 307 or Mazda 626 can ever hope to match. The cars on view were parked as the demolition of the Goree, a row of late 18th century warehouses, was nearing its final moments. In the early 1700s most of Britain's slave merchants were from London and Bristol. However, Liverpool merchants were increasingly involved and from about 1740 were outstripping their rivals. The Goree was named after an island off Dakar, Senegal in West Africa, one of the trading places for slaves. It is said that iron rings set into the walls here were used to secure slaves.

Liverpool Libraries and Information Services

Left: This must have been the view of Lord Street that a Luftwaffe pilot had as he flew towards Church Street and dropped his deadly load on the city beneath his wings. In 1949 evidence of the carnage wrought by enemy action was still very apparent. Great tracts of land lay waste and derelict buildings awaited the last rites of the demolition man's attention. Eventually, new offices and hotels, such as those now housing Radio Merseyside and the Moat House Hotel, would appear, but this reminder of the effect of modern warfare stayed with us for a long time after hostilities had formally ended. After the euphoria of VE and VJ Day had died down some people wondered out loud as to what we had achieved in our victory. Four years on and the rebuilding of the nation seemed to be happening at a snail's pace. Ration books, identity cards and a financial crisis were all with us. The pound was devalued, Berlin was blockaded until the middle of the year, the Communists took control in China and Russia tested the atom bomb. Those bluebirds over the white cliffs were not flying quite as high as they had done. George Orwell published his controversial '1984', with its message about 'big brother' and some of his ideas did not seem all that far off the mark.

Above: This view of Elliot Street was photographed from the roof of Blackler's buildings in 1962. Capstan can advertise their cigarettes in a day when the majority were smokers and there was no ban on advertising tobacco. The sign for the Forum cinema can just be seen. The film 'A Kind Of Loving' came out this year. If you stayed at home to watch television, there was a new programme about the police combating crime in their 'Z-Cars'. 'Danger Man', '77 Sunset Strip' and Perry Mason' were imported from America to provide further food for the crime hungry viewers. Television was being transmitted live from the States to Britain for the first time this year. The images were bounced off a sapphire studded satellite called Telstar, the world's first communications satellite. The years of austerity were ended and the people wanted the goods available in Blackler's shop and other stores like it. They wanted their family cars and their holidays to Southport and further. Even abroad. They wanted these things and they wanted them now. They would buy on the 'Never Never', as hire purchase was called. 'Live Now, Pay Later' was the title of a film. This attitude could also have been due to the fact that they were living in times when the threat of nuclear war was very real. The Americans had set up a blockade around Cuba, where the Russians had placed missiles aimed at America. Whatever the reason it was good to shop in Liverpool.

Events & occasions

Below: Did anybody ever enjoy the physical education lesson when they were at school? How many mothers came under serious pressure, from their offspring, to write a note asking for them to be excused the lesson? Many a cough had mysteriously developed during the previous night. The name for this lesson on the curriculum may have changed many times over the years, but the content has remained the same. The teachers' names may have been different, but they all believed that fresh-air, followed by perspiration, cold showers and goose-pimples, were for some reason good for you. Do you remember the cross-country run? The popular myth amongst children was that the teacher watched their progress around the course through a pair of binoculars from the roof of the school. The boys always managed to hide and enjoy a shared Woodbine. The danger of being caught added to the excitement.

It was fine if you liked milk, or orange juice in the infants, but it was torture to those who did not, when they were made to drink it every day.

In the newspaper article, on the nineteenth of May 1938, it was reported that 'a thousand children gave a display of physical drill, at Wavertree playground'. 'Drill' seems like the best word ever used for this activity. It was considered important that we were all spaced at equal distance apart. With the fingers of our right hands on the left shoulder of the person next to us, we shuffled in little steps until we formed straight and uniform lines. Each and every one of the thousand knew that the King and Queen were noticing how much better than the rest they were at pointing their toes.

Liverpool Libraries and Information Services

The showers stopped long enough for Elizabeth the Queen Mother to inspect the proud soldiers, who stood to attention with bayonets fixed. Their commander, who carries his sword over his shoulder, accompanies her. How smart they look. Over in America there was a new phenomenon of liberal individuals who talked about things being 'groovy' and 'hip'. No long haired 'beatniks' here. We definitely 'dig' the way these lads look.

She was in Liverpool primarily to invest a plaque to commemorate the start of the rebuilding of the Brown Library, which had been destroyed in the blitz. It was also a part of the 750th anniversary of the granting of King John's Charter to Liverpool.

The Queen Mother was no stranger to Liverpool. She and her husband, King George VI, had been in Liverpool in 1942 to meet naval personnel and merchant seamen. They appreciated the risks those men took in the Battle of the Atlantic. They were the sailors who risked everything to keep supply lines open. The crossing to America was a perilous one because of the constant threat of attack from U-boats. She was to return in 1959 to launch the Union Castle liner 'Windsor Castle'. It was the largest ship of its kind to be built in Britain since the war.

She and her husband King George worked hard to keep up the spirits of the people during the difficult years of war. King George is reputed to have said, when Buckingham Palace suffered some damage during an air raid on London, that he was glad that his home had been hit because he could talk to the people on more equal terms.

Left: In 1948 a party of naval visitors came to the English Electric factory to see at first hand the work taking place on the shop floor. It was too good an opportunity for some of them to miss when they encountered such a bevy of beauty sitting at the workbenches. There were some neat chat up lines being used and one sailor made sure that he got a chaste cuddle with one of the prettiest girls around. Fifty years later he would probably be done for sexual harassment, but back then it was innocent and natural behaviour and who could possibly object to that? Certainly not the recipient of the attention as she enjoyed the flattery. We seem to have lost all sense of proportion in our modern obsession with political correctness. English Electric was formed in 1918 from the merger of a number of companies in the heavy electrical industry. This gave it a capital of £5 million, more than any other British electrical company at the time. Although English Electric made a modest profit in its early years it struggled to keep its head above water during the depression of the late 1920s and early 1930s. However, in 1936 it began supplying trains and in 1938, as the country prepared for war, it moved into aircraft manufacture at the Government's request. This helped the company achieve record profits and was part of its contribution to the national effort. By the late 1940s English Electric had become one of the largest engineering companies in the country.

Below: Some companies are all profit margins and big business, but others have a more human side. English Electric knew all about balance sheets but it was also well aware that there were other things in life. The company hosted regular shows and entertainments for its workers and the community. In this case it was the turn of underprivileged children to benefit when they attended the 'Orphans' Christmas Party'. Life had dealt these nippers a raw deal and a chance for them to join the land of plenty was something that they would cherish for a long time. Several of the girls seem to have benefited from a job lot in flowered dress material, but that did not inhibit their excitement in being able to don party frocks and pose for the camera as Father Christmas was about to make a grand entry. There were crackers to be pulled, silly jokes to be read, mince pies to be scoffed and musical bumps to be played, but they were only the overture to the grand event. When the white haired present giver appeared in the doorway dozens of throats let rip a huge roar that would have rivalled any heard on the Kop when Roger Hunt found the back of the net. How the children treasured the magic colouring books they received, but how better they valued the memories of the day.

Below: One hundred and thirty two feet above the traffic and cars parked in St George's Plateau, the Duke of Wellington gazes down with a critical eye on the bunting which adorns his column. Maybe he agrees that the Festival of Britain is a good idea to shake off the gloom of the hardships still being faced in 1951. It was hoped it would be good for the economy to show the world what the nation was capable of producing. If it did nothing else but boost morale, then wasn't that a good idea? The festival in London was a surprising success, even to the organisers. Over eight million people paid it a visit.
Liverpool is blessed with some elegant buildings. Out of the picture are the Walker Gallery, the Central Library, and the Liverpool Museum, all magnificent in their own way. Adorned with a flag, the proud Sessions House can be seen in this photograph. Alongside it is Rushworth and Dreaper. Once this was a high-class music shop. They sold fine pianos, music, radiograms and record players. Sadly now many buildings in this picture have been demolished.

It is strange how, with the passage of time all things become treasures, and as they disappear their passing is mourned. The pedestrians don't give the parked cars a second glance, unless to worry about the problems their increasing numbers will bring to the city. Yet now we see them as a row of 'classics'. Even Pickford's removal van has a certain charm to the modern eye.

Liverpool Libraries and Information Services

Even covered in soot and grime, St George's Hall is an elegant, beautiful classic building. It is not too grand that the Punch and Judy show cannot perform in front of its portico. Liverpool is a city of such contrasting images. 'Professor Codman's Punch and Judy Show was an almost permanent feature here at one time. Imagine that Punch and Judy shows had never existed, and the idea was new and was being presented to the producer of a modern children's television show. 'This is the plot. There is this man called Punch, who talks through his nose. His wife, Judy, asks him to look after the baby. He hits the baby with a big stick and feeds it to a crocodile. The crocodile frightens all the children who are watching.

Then Judy returns and Punch hits her over the head with his stick. The police arrive and he tries to hit them too. They capture him however, and Judy recovers from concussion, the crocodile is made to cough up the baby, and they all live happily ever after'. The script would be condemned as violent, and anti-social. It would cause the children to have nightmares, and grow into violent anti-social individuals themselves. It is strange that the show has continued to be popular with both parents and children for decades.

The little Shirley Temple on dad's shoulders seems healthy and well adjusted, despite their exposure to the violence of Punch. Could this be due to a diet of fish and fresh vegetables?

Above: The Top Hat Record Bar on Dale Street was one of the favourite haunts of pop stars, or recording artists as they were known in 1957, wanting to promote a record or appearance at a local theatre. The bemused object of the autograph hunters, looking very dapper in his sharp suit and wavy, Brylcreemed hair, was a relative newcomer to fame. Lonnie Donegan was one of the first beneficiaries of the spending power of that new phenomenon, the teenager. Unlike many modern acts, Donegan had served an apprenticeship as a musician with the very best. Lonnie played banjo and guitar with the Chris Barber Jazz Band before becoming a star in his own right with 'Rock Island Line', a top 10 hit in 1956. He was the first British male to have a pair of top 10 hits in America. Known as the 'King of Skiffle', he blended jazz, blues and comedy in a recording career that gave him a string of hits over a six year period. With a repertoire that included 'Battle of New Orleans', 'My Old Man's a Dustman' and 'The Party's Over' he was ensured a lifelong following even after the hit singles dried up. To underline his popularity, Lonnie appeared on the Jools Holland TV show with Van Morrison in 2000 and an album they recorded together went into the top 20. By then he was pushing 70.

Right: Time is frozen as the shutter snaps to record the Earl of Derby about to bring down his bat to make contact with the ball. His posture is good, and he is keeping his eye on the target. Whether he did make a good strike is not recorded, but the official opening of the Speke recreation ground on the 7th July 1958 certainly is. Aeroplanes coming in to land at Liverpool airport may not be in any danger, but the improperly dressed gentleman at square leg may be in for a shock. The windows of the prefabs on the border of the playing field could also be within range. The prefabricated buildings, lined in neat rows, may not be as grand as the not-too-distant Speke Hall, but their occupants grew fond of the practical little dwellings. They were compact and cosy. Considering that they were originally regarded as a very temporary measure to solve the post war housing shortage, there are still some to be seen in different parts of the country even today. The standard parts were manufactured on the assembly line principle and transported to the sites, where the bases and utilities had been laid to receive them. They were erected, and ready for occupation, in a very short time. Once dad had planted the garden, and mother had made the curtains and filled the home with the simple utility furniture, the bungalow took on an individual character and became a home. There is a legend that monks from Birkenhead Priory, escaping from the soldiers of Henry VIII with the priory's treasure, dug a tunnel to Speke. The tunnel collapsed, entombing them. Could this have been the first Mersey tunnel?

Below: 'Ignore the camera and look natural', was the photographer's instruction during the Libraries Committee Inspection in September 1955. These were the fifties, when 'teenagers' were invented and your hair had to be in a 'quiff' at the front. It was the closest mum would let you get to an Elvis haircut. Short back and sides was somehow healthier. Adults seemed to think that hair combed into a DA meant that a boy would suddenly rebel, dress as a 'Teddy Boy', and develop anti-social habits. There are many good books to be found on the shelves of the library, which would be fine for a growing boy. The new book, 'The Diary of Anne Frank', would give them an interesting insight into life in an occupied country, but most of these boys, were they offered a choice, would opt for another publication out this year, 'Lolita'. Then, in 1955, came Bill Haley with a 'kiss curl' of hair plastered to his brow. 'Rock and Roll' had arrived. 'Rock Around the Clock' was causing riots in cinemas, and many town councils were banning it. The ballroom, with its etiquette of politely asking a girl for the 'pleasure of the next dance' was disappearing, along with the sound of Ruby Murray singing 'Softly, Softly'. Whilst, in contrast, Liverpool's Frankie Vaughan sang romantic songs to the ladies offering them the moonlight. David Whitfield, Dickie Valentine, Alma Cogan and many others sent forth messages like, 'Love and marriage go together like a horse and Carriage', and Frank Sinatra threw coins into a fountain and fell in love - all good wholesome stuff!

Above: The little lad does not really know why he is clutching the union flag but in 1962 we were all true royalists and flocked in droves to see a real princess in the flesh. It was not the warmest of days so people were well wrapped up as a drop of rain or a chilly breeze was not going to stop them from greeting their special guest. Princess Alexandra was inspecting the guard of honour provided by the Deva cadets. She has represented the Queen on numerous occasions, acting as a Counsellor of State in Her Majesty's absence abroad. In addition, she has made many official visits overseas, often accompanied by her husband, Angus Ogilvy, whom she married on 24 April 1963 in Westminster Abbey. HRH Princess Alexandra is the Queen's first cousin and daughter of Princess Marina, another popular figure in royal circles. As a young woman Princess Alexandra made sure that she would have a wider knowledge of the world than some of her peers had. On completing her education she took a

nursing course at Great Ormond Street Hospital before starting to undertake official engagements. Her involvement in medicine has led to patronages that reflect this interest. She is the deputy president of the British Red Cross Society and the patron of the Alzheimer's Society, St Christopher's Hospice and Queen Alexandra's Royal Naval Nursing Service.

Top right: At five and twenty minutes to eleven a young Princess Margaret confidently addresses the Liverpool City Council in the oak panelled rooms. Sitting alongside of her was the Mayor of Liverpool, Alderman Bewley CBE JP. Everyone wears the serious looks befitting such a solemn occasion. It is the Princess's duty to inaugurate Liverpool's Commonwealth weeks. Later, in the Brown Library, she officially opened the commonwealth library. The people still sympathised with her even though two years had elapsed since her romance with the handsome, Group Captain Peter Townsend, had come to an end. She had wanted to marry the former equerry to the late king, but he was considered 'unsuitable' as he was a divorcee. As she was in line of succession to the throne, and the queen was head of the Church of England, which taught that marriage is indissoluble, she could not reconcile herself to a civil marriage. The forced abdication of her uncle, Edward VIII, because he wished to marry a divorcee, Mrs Wallis Simpson, was still remembered. That was the end to a sad fairy-tale story of a Princess who wished to marry the handsome soldier.

It raised a considerable amount of debate at a time when marriage was sacrosanct. Or was it? Divorce rates had been steadily climbing throughout the fifties. Many women wanted to be more like Brigitte Bardot, and less like Doris Day. By 1959 more than a third of all married women had returned to work and were enjoying greater freedoms. Grace Metalious wrote a book about the unsatisfied desires of the housewives of a small American town, 'Peyton Place'.

Liverpool Libraries and Information Services

Liverpool Libraries and Information Services

PEDESTRIANS
USE OTHER
FOOTWALK ➔

Left: The cameras and the people wait patiently for the arrival of the Queen and the Duke of Edinburgh on this fine June day in 1977. This was the Queen's Silver Jubilee year. Schools have been closed for the day and many businesses have declared a holiday. The office windows provide a fine vantage point to see the royal party and their entourage who will be arriving aboard the Royal Yacht Britannia. Throughout the city were 'scenes', the first of which was a musical pageant at the Metropolitan Cathedral. There were others in Hope Street with a finale at the Anglican Cathedral. The Queen and Prince Philip cruised the Mersey on 'Royal Iris' before returning to the Royal Yacht Britannia. Those not able to be here will be able to see the event on television. Cameras of this size were in fixed, though well-chosen, locations. How splendid the buildings look after they were stripped of the coat of soot and grime. The liver birds have welcomed all ships to the port for many years. Made of copper and standing 18ft high they are easily spotted as a ship approaches this well known dock. The clocks are out

Liverpool Libraries and Information Services

of the picture, so we do not know how much longer the camera crew and crews have to wait. Perhaps they are not aware that the giant clocks, on the towers of this elegant building, are bigger than those of Big Ben. They are 25ft in diameter. The minute hands are 14ft long. The flag is flying above its next-door neighbour, the former headquarters of the Cunard Company.

Above left: The crowds turned out on this lovely sunny day to see the Queen and the Duke of Edinburgh. A guard stands prepared to give a gun salute if required to do so, and several lucky school children have the perfect spot from which to observe the Royal party. This year she celebrated the Silver Jubilee of her Reign, and the people have put out the flags to give her thanks, and to wish her well. The Right Reverend David Sheppard, Bishop of Liverpool, leads them up the steps to the Anglican Cathedral. Following the Duke are the Lord Mayor and Lady Mayoress of Liverpool, Councillor and Mrs Paul Orr. The Queen must have been thinking of other visits she had made to this great Anglican Cathedral. Shortly after the end of the war she, then a Princess, and her then new husband Prince Philip, had officially unlocked the Central Door. King Edward VII had laid the foundation stone in 1904. Gilbert Giles Scott, who was only in his early twenties when the work was entrusted to him, designed this building. King George V had attended the consecration of the Cathedral in 1924. The Queen was only a young girl when her uncle, Edward VIII, abdicated in order to

marry Mrs Simpson. Not only did this have great significance for her father, who now became king, but also for herself and the new expectations of her. Although many people refused to believe it, a 'King' of a different kind died in 1977. Elvis Presley died at his home in Memphis, aged forty-two.

Top: The band of the Queen's Lancashire Regiment strike up a rousing tune, alongside the frigate HMS Tartar. The flags spell out a message of welcome to the Queen and the Duke of Edinburgh as they visited Liverpool on the 21st June 1977. The port is no stranger to ships of size. In the early 1900s, the port saw many Cunard and White Star liners who plied their way across the Atlantic. In 1907 many thousands turned out to see the Lusitania begin her maiden voyage to New York. She made a record crossing of four days, nineteen hours and fifty-two minutes. This was a record to be broken four years later by the Mauretania in a time nine hours and eleven minutes less.

These docks saw the landing of many American soldiers, for whom Liverpool was their first taste of England. They were billeted with families, who had little choice in the matter, and, speaking of taste, asked for coffee! We didn't drink coffee, not even if it had been available. They soon acquired a taste for our tea. They had been told that all the people in England were starving, and had been given instructions not to accept food. But they were given the hospitality normally given. Bread, margarine, ham and cheese, or similar, would have been provided. They returned the compliment with things from their stores. Soon food parcels began arriving in response to the letters sent home by these soldiers. Some contained cakes covered with icing sugar and desiccated coconut. What a luxury!

Making a marque in Liverpool

What goes around comes around and for Jaguar this meant a return to its northern roots as the new millennium got under way. There had been some production of Jaguar body panels at Ford's Halewood during the 1990s, but it was the coming of the 21st century that cemented a major change for the plant. The company had already greeted the dawn of the new era with the announcement that it was to enter the heady world of Formula One Grand Prix racing for the first time. But it was the revelation of plans for a new sports saloon, a compact 2.5 or 3 litre model to be known as the X-Type, that provided Halewood with a new impetus. This state of the art car would be the smallest that Jaguar had produced in 30 years and had the benefit of permanent four wheel drive. Any younger car buyer wanting to be a part of the Jaguar experience would have the sheer joy of wallowing in the luxury of the X-Type's stylish and contemporary design. Backed by nimble driving dynamics the car illustrates all that is best in advanced engineering and intuitive know-how.

To achieve such a result meant establishing a new Jaguar plant aswell as the one at Coventry, home to Jaguar since before the war. The company injected £300 million into an imaginative refurbishment programme that has completely revitalised and reshaped the old plant. The refurbishment was essential for future success as for 30 years Halewood had been producing Ford Escorts and it was essential that quality levels had to be raised to produce a quality vehicle like the Jaguar. All this has been achieved with the replacement of most of the former production facilities by the world class quality levels necessary in delivering what is commensurate with the creation of a premium sports saloon. Halewood has now provided Jaguar with all the major production facilities on one site, a state of affairs it had not had before. All the main elements of press shop, body construction, paint shop and the trim and final assembly lines are laid out in an organised, linked manner next to one another to guarantee a smoothly flowing production line. A new

Above: The Jaguar X-Type, manufactured at Halewood. **Below:** *The Administration block at Jaguar Halewood nearing completion.* **Right:** *The refurbished administration building which was completed in 2001.*

The working culture at Halewood has been dramatically changed in line with the transformation of the production processes. The technical training centre has the responsibility for educating apprentices, but the company's training of the workforce goes much further. There is a close working relationship with Liverpool John Moores University that provides appropriate courses for shop floor workers, engineers and managerial staff, some of them to degree level. As the plant moved into Jaguar production all employees underwent extensive retraining to equip them with the up to date knowledge that enabled them to adapt to the demands of building a top notch quality car. It was not enough to change the equipment and processes, a culture change within Halewood had to be achieved. Over one million hours of training, most of it on site, was given to the workforce, averaging some 350 hours for each and every employee. This had the effect of recharging the workers' batteries as well as those under the bonnets of the X-Types that began to roll off the assembly lines in February 2001. With a capacity for the manufacture of 100,000 vehicles each year Jaguar has more than begun a new chapter in its life story. It has probably started another edition.

supplier park alongside has added to the efficiency of the 65 acre site that has been created in co-operation with the Speke Garston Development Company and English Partnerships. This has seen the development of the Boulevard Industry Park, built on the original Halewood site, creating about 500 jobs and enabling important suppliers such as Conix, Lear, Infast, Stadco and Visteon to manufacture components on Jaguar's doorstep. This seamless supplier network feeds components and sub-assemblies into the production line in an efficient and 'just in time' process.

*Top, **both pictures:** X-Types in production.*
***Right:** A Jaguar X-Type in the spray-paint booth.*

The birth of Jaguar

It was in 1935 that the Jaguar name first came to the notice of the British public when William Lyons unveiled a new range of cars at the Motor Show. Born in Blackpool in 1901, he had worked as a car salesman in the pioneering days of motoring. In keeping with most young men of the early 20th century Lyons was fascinated by the developments in the burgeoning world of transport. Whilst others followed aeronautical interests he kept his feet firmly on the ground in all senses of the phrase. His love of speed was initially satisfied by the various nippy motorbikes that he owned. One of his neighbours, William Walmsley, had a similar passion for whizzing along the roads leading into the coastal resort. In a modest venture Walmsley had begun to produce sidecars. After purchasing one of these Lyons persuaded his neighbour to join forces with him in a business partnership. In 1922 their Swallow sidecar was an immediate hit. Despite his personal preference for motorbikes Lyons was a shrewd enough businessman to realise that four wheeled transport was where the major profits lay. He decided to move into car manufacture and used an Austin Seven chassis as the base for the first stylish body that he produced. The Austin Seven Swallow was introduced to the nation in 1927, generating one order of 500 models from a London distributor. Lyons' little Blackpool factory was a victim of its own success, being too small to be able to cope with demand. Within a year the Swallow company had relocated to Coventry, the very heartland of the motor industry in this country. An alliance was forged

with the Standard Motor Company that saw Lyons manufacturing and marketing his own cars, fitted with Standard engines and other components. His SSI, selling for £310 but looking like £1,000, according to the press, did not just look the part with its low slung body, sleek lines and long bonnet. It performed superbly as well. In 1934 the touring version won the team prize in the Alpine International Trial.

By now his ambitious and revolutionary ideas were about to send him along a path that would put his cars at the top of every person's ideal shopping list. Lyons had a new chassis ready and a magnificently powerful six cylinder overhead valve engine, capable of delivering 2.5 litres of unbridled power. An elegantly striking saloon body topped off the new concept in luxury and performance. Having decided that a new look demanded a new name Lyons considered a number of possibilities drawn from the ranks of a variety of creatures. As his new car was definitely neither fish nor fowl he looked for something that would suggest a balance of power, grace and speed. Not surprisingly he turned to the feline world for inspiration and the emotive Jaguar name and insignia came into being. Journalists at the Motor Show were staggered when it was announced that the SS Jaguar, such a prestigious looking machine, was to be marketed for just £385 as they had estimated that the cost would be over £600. This new range of cars included the first true sports car, the SS Jaguar 100, which won the team prize in the 1937 RAC Rally. A 3.5 litre version, produced in 1938, could go from 0-60 mph in 10.5 seconds and had a top speed of over 100 mph. By the start of the war Jaguar production had reached 5,000.

Top centre: Jaguar's founder, Sir William Lyons. **Above left:** *An advertisement for one of Lyons' Swallow Sidecars.* **Right:** *The launch of the SS Jaguar in 1935.*

The Second World War

During the war Lyons' first production items regained their popularity. They had become less and less important in time, but sidecars were back in demand, particularly for military use. Jaguar also had some involvement in aircraft manufacture and repair work, experience that would stand it in good stead for future developments once the war was over. The XK120, one of the finest sports cars

ever built, was unveiled in 1948. It could reach speeds in excess of 120 mph and so captured international interest that orders flooded in from abroad, with the USA being a major customer base. The company went from strength to strength in the 1950s as its profile continued to be raised. Hollywood stars drove Jaguar models and both the Queen Mother and the Duke of Kent were particular enthusiasts. Britain's top racing driver, Stirling Moss, had a legendary partnership with the company, driving Jaguar cars to success in countless saloon races, rallies and tourist trophies. The racing version had spectacular victories in the 24 hour Le Mans race, dominating this famous event throughout the decade. In 1956 William Lyons received a knighthood for his services to the nation's exports, but everyone knew that his cars' successes in lifting trophies on the road and the track had a lot to do with the honour bestowed upon him by the Queen. Sir William, as he now was, retired from business after 50 years at the helm of his company. By then Jaguar had merged with BMC, a move that was followed just two years later in 1968 by a further merger with Leyland, creating the British Leyland Group. Sir William

Above: *Whitley bombers, essential wartime production at Jaguar's Coventry site.* ***Below:*** *The Jaguar 2.4 Litre Saloon, 1959.*

remained as the honorary president of Jaguar after his retirement and maintained a keen interest in events up to his death in 1985.

The growth of Halewood

Lyons would have been pleased with the recent developments that brought his company back to the region of his birth. However, the area had changed a lot from the days when his Swallows first flew their Blackpool nest. Speke Airport, or Liverpool John Lennon Airport as it now is, was but a quiet outpost and the whole district around Halewood was semi rural. However, after the war there was a large increase in population here, but few jobs to go with it and unemployment ran at unacceptable levels in a country that the prime minister, Harold Macmillan, told us had never had it so good. The decision of the Ford Motor Company to open a site for car production here provided a shot in the arm for the local economy. Thanks should be given in part to the government for it had been used as sounding-out

board by Ford in its search for an appropriate location. There had been a decline in traditional labour intensive industrial and commercial businesses. Encouragement was given to companies to invest in depressed areas and Merseyside, with its 27,000 unemployed, fitted the bill. Construction was begun in 1960 and, by 1962, the training of the first recruits to the new workforce had commenced. A hangar at the airport was turned into a training centre. Some 250 supervisors were moved from Dagenham to undertake the education of the new employees. A mock assembly line containing the shells of 10 Anglias and 10 Populars was set up as the first 25 hourly paid and five salaried staff took up their posts on 1 January 1962.

Top: The C-Type at Le Mans in 1953. **Above right:** *The 1962 SI 3.8 E-Type.* **Left:** *One of the first Ford Anglia's to leave the production line at Ford Halewood.*

as it once had been. That very first car is now kept in Liverpool Museum for all to see. All those early cars built here were the 997cc Anglias that had that distinctive reverse sloping back window, though the Corsair (1963-70) was the first new model to be built exclusively at Halewood. The Halewood site was purchased from Liverpool Corporation and the British Transport Commission. More than 2 million tons of earth were shifted, but not without controversy as two ancient moated sites, the Old Hutt and Wright's Moat, were destroyed in the process. The gigantic nature of the work can be gauged from considering some of the figures involved. Structural steel weighed 40,000 tons, 300,000 tons of concrete was needed, 4 million bricks used, 2 million square feet of roofing erected and 50,000 gallons of paint applied. Little wonder that the cost of the initial operation came to £38 million. A further investment in the plant of a £17.5 million expansion scheme brought about the opening of the Transmission Plant in 1964. Nearly 1,800 machines were transferred from Dagenham so that transmission production for the Zephyr, Zodiac, Anglia and Cortina models could take place. Other notable milestones in this decade included the production of the 500,000th car, a Corsair, in 1965, extensions to the transmission plant, the opening of the new panel storage building and the press line starting production. But it was with the launch of new models that most members of the public were

The whole exercise cost £1 million, but proved to be a valuable investment over the next 40 years. The ceremonial tape was cut on 8 March 1963 at the official opening and the honour of being the first car to see the light of day at Halewood fell to a lime green Ford Anglia 105E De Luxe. The Lord Mayor of Liverpool sat behind the wheel of one of the models that was to be a popular family saloon for many of us as motor car ownership became the norm during the 1960s, rather than the preserve of the middle classes

*Top left: Celebrating the production of four million cars at Halewood. **Above left:** The one millionth Ford Escort produced at the plant. **Right:** Staff training taking place in Halewood's Technical Training Centre.*

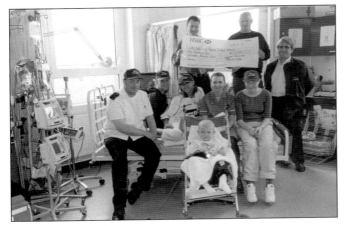

facelift two years later. By this time Halewood had built five million vehicles, passing that magic figure in 1991.

Jaguar comes to Halewood

Whilst the Halewood plant had been moving forward Jaguar had lost some of its identity and image after the British Leyland merger and virtual state control. The Thatcher government made plans to privatise a number of industries and in August 1984 Jaguar shares were floated on the London Stock Exchange. The company entered a period when it rediscovered itself, achieving considerable success in the growth and development of its business. Plans were laid to manufacture its own body panels through a joint venture with GKN, leading to the formation of Venture Pressings. Another joint venture, JaguarSport, was created to produce and market sporting versions of Jaguar saloons and high performance sports cars. The outstanding XJ220 and XJR-

interested, with perhaps one of the most memorable coming along in 1968. The Ford Escort was to be the mainstay of the home market for the next three decades. Within five years of its launch the millionth Escort came off the Halewood production line. By 1975 it was Europe's top selling car and a Mark II version had been launched. Investment of £205 million for the building of the Mark III model in 1980 helped the Escort win the European Car of the Year Award. Ten years later another investment programme, this time of £600 million, led to a revamped new Escort being introduced into the market, followed by a major

Top left: *Jaguar staff presenting a cheque to Alder Hey Children's Hospital.* **Above left:** *Jaguar employees taking part in a Community Environment scheme at Halewood Country Park.* **Above right:** *The Jaguar X-TYPE nearing the end of the production line.* **Right:** *The imposing facade of Halewood, 2002.* **Below:** *The Lord Mayor of Knowsley receives a ceremonial mace, made by apprentices at Halewood.*

15 were included in the results of this successful enterprise. By 1993 the production of body panels for Jaguar had begun at Halewood, the plant becoming the first in Europe to achieve ISO9000. By 1998 Halewood had been designated as the production site for Jaguar's new 'baby', the X-Type series. Work began on transforming the work practices and culture of the site. Its cars had an incredible turning circle, but it was the production at Halewood that required a complete about face. A programme designated as 'The Halewood Difference' was instituted, under the guidance of Senn Delaney Leadership, a top consultancy firm. Within 18 months of its launch in December 1998 there was a 20 per cent rise in productivity under the new management team that had David Hudson as Plant Operations Director. Hudson had a reputation for making things happen and he refused to allow the problems to fester. People were encouraged to bring those problems to him rather than let them remain unspoken or be part of a whispering campaign. Employees were encouraged to be part of the change and to play a role within the reshaping needed at Halewood so that they were contributing to what was

happening and did not feel that they were having something foisted upon them. Issues were dealt with head on.

Word soon spread that there was something fresh and approachable about this company's

style, without losing its sense of purpose and resolve. Even to a casual visitor the difference was immediately visible in the working environment. Halewood became a cleaner and more pleasant place to be, helping raise morale and improve quality, self esteem and safety. In the end it is the customer who benefits with quality service from a quality product. When the last Ford left Halewood in 2000 it had become the 'Escort with Jag quality'.

The Jaguar attitude to life is not just about the quality of its machines but also the company's integration within the community and care for the environment. At Halewood new state of the art spray booths use water based colours, reducing solvent emission. New heater and incineration systems have yielded major reductions in carbon monoxide and similar noxious gases. Jaguar has set out in a systematic and thoughtful way to win the hearts and minds of people. The change at Halewood came from within, making Jaguar's move there a success, but one only achieved by a mixture of the determination and vision practised by modern management, just as William Lyons showed over three quarters of a century ago.

Top right: *X-Type's leaving Halewood via the new railhead that has been established there.* ***Above left:*** *The then Managing Director, Jonathan Browning, at the opening of the Halewood Railhead in 2001.* ***Left:*** *The new X-Type pictured in Liverpool.*

At leisure

Elsewhere the baby show was attracting entries from proud mothers who believed that their offspring were the cutest the world had ever seen. Scrubbed up to look like a cross between Shirley Temple and Bubbles, the Pear's girl, youngsters were dressed in all manner of improbable finery to try to catch the judge's eye. The final decision always thrilled one mother and, at best, irritated scores of others. The English Electric Show was one of the high spots of the 1940s and a ride on the model train was a must for boys and girls who had queued for a long time to get their turn. Notice how many dads are looking on at the scene. Oh how they wished that they were in short trousers once more. If only one of them had been brave enough to take his place on the train then all the other fathers would have followed suit. What they would have given to trade places with the engine driver and stoke the boiler, toot the whistle and open the valve that set the locomotive in motion. There has not been a man born yet who can walk past a toyshop without pausing to look in the window and try to spot a Dinky car or an Airfix biplane. Girls grow into women but little boys just get larger.

It was hardly the London Eye, but in 1948 this Big Wheel at New Brighton was scary enough for most of us. Nowadays, youngsters think nothing of roller coaster rides like the Colossus or the gravity defying Shockwave, but their horizons were closer just after the war. Who is to say that the rides were any less enjoyable than those we have today? In the fairground we had the caterpillar ride where a cover was gently lowered over passengers as the machine made its wiggly way around a small circuit. Girls shyly cuddled up to their sweethearts, safe in the knowledge that for a few minutes they were out of the way of mum's prying eyes. Then it was off to the Ghost Train where make believe cobwebs and odd looking skeletons dangled from the ceiling in an attempt to make a lass squeal and cling onto her escort that little bit tighter. Swing boats, hoop-la and coconuts stuck onto shies with the postwar equivalent of superglue were part of the fun of the fair. Sticky candyfloss and gooey toffee apples that rotted your teeth and made you an early candidate for NHS dental treatment were all part of the occasion. It was always a laugh to see some weedy youth trying to swing a hammer that would shoot an object up a pole and ring the bell. He never managed it. Meanwhile, back on the Big Wheel a woman wearing a coat made from hamster fur was causing problems when she refused to get off.

Above: The second world war ended and the nation flocked to venues that offered entertainment that was such a contrast to the miserable days of the first half of the 1940s. Soccer stadiums were filled, queues formed outside grounds to watch county cricket, cinemas were packed and variety halls had house full notices. At New Brighton Wilkie's Circus put on two shows a day, with three on Saturdays. Inside the arena the ringmaster cracked his whip and we cracked our sides with laughter at the antics of the clowns. We knew that bucket they had was full of confetti and not water, but we ducked and squealed just the same when they threw the contents at us. It was fascinating to watch dad's eyes come out on stalks when that sequinned girl rode round the ring on a horse that sported a gorgeous white plume in its headdress. We had no idea that our father was so interested in equestrianism. Perhaps he was worried that the rider might catch cold as she did not seem to be wearing very much. Performing sealions, playing 'Rule Britannia' on motor horns, dogs on seesaws, roaring lions and elephants rising up on their hind legs were magical moments that gave us so many joyous memories. There were thrills galore up above our heads as trapeze artists caught one another in mid air and tightrope walkers tiptoed their way along a cable that seemed no thicker than a cotton thread.

Below: Before the ozone layer started to develop as many holes as Aunt Maggie's stockings we had proper seasons. It was foggy in the autumn, cold in the winter, damp in spring, but in the summer the sun shone brightly. In the 1930s a trek out to the beach and pool at West Kirby was a real adventure. Buckets and spades, fishing nets and a little flag to stick on top of a sandcastle was all the equipment we needed for a great day out. Mum made the sarnies and dad got his knotted hanky ready to pop on his head during a spot of snoozing on a corporation deckchair. Once on the sands we claimed our little bit of space and marked out our territory by digging a small pit in which to sit. Mum rolled her skirt up to her knees and we covered her legs in sand, only releasing her if she promised to let us go to the 'stop me and buy one' ice cream tricycle that was on its way along the prom. Donkeys plodded up and down the front carrying little tots who tried to persuade their parents to let them have another go. Punch and Judy, pierrot shows and sand sculpture artists offered free entertainment and an escape from the reality of the depression years that meant money was tight and jobs scarce.

Above: When Ernest Evans asked whether it was a bird or a plane up there and answered himself by telling us that it was a twister, a craze was born that swept dance floors across the western world. He also made sure that countless numbers of children would be embarrassed at weddings, 21st dos and parties during the 1990s as their parents risked hernias and heart attacks attempting to twist the night away whilst their offspring raised their eyes to heaven. Evans was a fan of the 1950s rocker Fats Domino and used his name as the inspiration for becoming known as Chubby Checker. Oddly, his first big hit in Britain was in 1961 with 'Let's Twist Again', a follow up to 'The Twist', a record that only became very popular the following year. By 1963, when this couple attempted to keep their seams straight as they gyrated in the front room to the

music from their Dansette record player, Chubby's star had already begun to wane. He switched to the limbo in an effort to promote another dance form, but with limited success. Re-issues of his twist records have enjoyed new popularity in the intervening years, but have only added to the cringe factor for those forced to watch this couple 40 years on as they take the floor to the sound of 'Twist and Shout' or 'Peppermint Twist'. Sit down, mum, it's so gross.

Facing page, centre: In 1963 the game of 'arrers was still a pub and club game, practised by men over a social pint on a night out with their mates. It was not until the great god of television took an interest in the News of the World and the Embassy Championships in the late 1970s that darts players became household names. Leighton Rees was one of the first superstars, followed by Eric Bristow and John Lowe. Viewers marvelled at Jocky Wilson's waistline and Bobby George's extravagant sequins, whilst mums sighed over the boyish looks of Keith Deller. Rod Harrington even brought ties back into fashion, but that was long after these Cammell Laird workers had collected their certificates and modest prizes awarded after the company's championships. The workforce turned out in large numbers to witness the ceremony and it must have been a proud day for these lads when their prowess on the oche was rewarded in front of their pals. In years to come they might have been able to bring their skills to Jim Bowen's TV show 'Bullseye', where accuracy with a tungsten tip, allied to rudimentary general knowledge, could win quaintly selected prizes. It always seemed a mystery as to why the winner of Bully's star prize got a petrol lawn mower when he lived on the tenth floor of a high rise block of flats.

Below: The boats, of the Mersey Motor Boat Club, are decorated with flags on this sunny day in 1962. Everyone is relaxing now that everything is ready for the event. 'Ship-shape and Bristol fashion'. Ladders are fixed to the roof. Are they there to provide a lookout point? Are they ready to meet a Royal Yacht, or the tall ships as they glide gracefully into the Mersey? These sailors may only be of 'amateur' status now, but many may have 'done their bit' in the Battle of the Atlantic. At least they will be able to boast a sailing heritage of some kind. One of the Captains of the QE2, Robin Woodall, came from Hoylake on the Wirral. These are the enthusiasts. No plastic 'Tupperware' boats for them. Only Clinker built and timber hulls, built around a keel, like the spine and ribs of a whale. Their craft are painted and varnished to a mirror finish. All brass fittings are gleaming in the sun, and the flags are spelling out a message of welcome. The estuary is no stranger to historic ships. In the sixties The British Argosy sailed in. At 107,729 tons she was the biggest, and the longest, ship ever to enter the Mersey. Many ships, like The Empress of Canada in April 1961, made their maiden voyages from Liverpool. She was a regular visitor until December 1971, when she made her last trip bearing that name. She returned in 1999 as the Apollo cruise ship. The port has been host to many war ships, including HMS Coventry, a type 42 destroyer, which sailed to the Falklands and was sunk by a bomb in 1982.

Above: When we got home, that day, we could hardly speak! We had shouted and sung at the top of our voices. As the open topped bus passed us, we sang those words, which are forged in iron above the Shankley gates at Anfield, 'You'll never walk alone'. We sang it then even louder than we sing it from the Kop during a match. I can still remember small things about that day. The bus fleet number was 186. Why such insignificant details should stick in the memory is a mystery. Maybe it is a measure of the importance of that day in our lives. We knew the bus was coming. Long before it came into view the noise heralded its arrival. I could see that deadly duo, Keegan and Toshak, Clemence was holding the cup high in his safe hands. Lawler, Lindsay, Smith, Lloyd, Hughes, Cormack

and Callaghan. There was Hall and Boersma with Heighway, for whom they had both substituted, one in each match. And in the middle, that little man who was in reality a giant for us, King Billy!

William Shankley had come to us from Huddersfield Town, who, after reaching the giddy heights of third in Division One in 1954, the same season that Liverpool had been relegated to Division Two, were now descending. Never the less they had played us in the 1958-59 season and beaten us 5-0, but we will say little of that!

Bill Shankley moved to Anfield the following year. In his first season he signed Roger Hunt, who turned out to be the most consistent goal scorer throughout the sixties. Now in 1973 the UEFA Cup came to Liverpool. Borussia Moenchengladbach had been worthy opponents. In the first game Keegan scored two, and Lloyd a third in the first half. In the second leg Borrusia came back fighting and were 2-0 up by half time. The Liverpool lads held on, and brought the cup home. Just like a story from the Hotspur comic book.

Bill Shankley is reported as having said, 'Football isn't a matter of life and death. It's much more important than that!' For us on this day we agreed with him!

Top: 'They're off!' was the cry in 1966, but they very nearly were not. Mrs Topham had announced, two years earlier, that she wished to sell the land for building development. Lord Sefton sought an injunction to prevent the sale from proceeding, as, he claimed, it was a breech of the original contract with Topham's Ltd. The legal wrangle continued, but Mrs Topham insisted that 1966 would be the last time that races would be held. William Lynn, in 1835, set aside October racing exclusively for hurdling. One hundred pounds was donated by an Alderman of Liverpool for the first Grand Liverpool Steeplechase, later to be called the Grand National. The winner of the first hurdle race was Captain Martin Beecher. He was thrown from his horse at the third fence, which has, ever since, borne his name.

This was a most interesting meeting in 1966. Less than an hour before the camera captured this picture, 'Drake's Drum' had caused a sensation by winning the six-furlong race, the Hulton Plate. The horse was led into the winner's enclosure by a longhaired pop star. A member of a group called the Beatles, Paul McCartney had bought the horse for his father.

In the Grand National, Mr Tim Durant rode his daughter's horse. What was surprising was that he was sixty-six years old at the time. The odds against him winning were a hundred to one.

The eventual winner was a horse called 'Battleship', owned by an American lady, Mrs Marion du Pont Scott. Many may have missed the fact that she was at the race with her husband Randolph Scott, the cowboy film star.

Wartime

Below: 'Scrap for Victory', says the government slogan. 'Save your scrap and win the scrap', 'Every scrap shortens the scrap', shouted the morale boosting messages. Now the 'rag and bone man', with his horse and cart, no longer shouted in the streets and offered the children a balloon in exchange. Now housewives and mothers were giving it willing for nothing if their was the slightest possibility that it would help to end the war and bring their men-folk home. They gave their kettles, saucepans, tin baths, and metal railings. It was no longer possible to import the raw materials required to produce weapons and ammunition so it was gathered from anywhere. Families returned home from the cinema, having been stirred by the Movie-tone News reports that all was going well, to discover that, not only the ornamental railings from the park had been taken, but also the ones from around their houses and their churches. During 1942 the Ministry of Works collected over one and a half million tons of gates and railings. There was 'The Great Aluminium Scare', when it was realised that it could not be imported. The Women's Voluntary Service went from door to door collecting. That's when the aluminium saucepans went. People gave gladly. It helped to feel that there was something one could do to have a direct influence on events. They may not have felt the same way had they known that much of it was never used.

THE STREETS

Lonnie Donnegan sang a song about his father. 'My old man's a dustman', he sang and told of his dad's 'gor blimey trousers'. It is doubtful that Lonnie's dad had a dustcart of the high tech variety such as this one operating in Liverpool in 1943. It was the 'Pagefield Refuse Container', with a circular barrel device, which compacted the rubbish. There is a tendency to think that recycling of waste and the care of disposal are modern concepts, but in 1943 everyone was aware of the importance of scrap for the war effort. The rubbish dump took on a whole new importance. The warning not to litter the streets was painted on the sides of all Liverpool's public vehicles. It seemed to work to some degree.

Imagine a conversation between these two men in 1943. 'What do you make of this new scheme for collecting your taxes then, 'arry?' What's that then Bill? "Stead of you telling them what you earn and they telling you what you owe, they're going to take the tax from your pay afore you get it. It's called 'pay as you earn". 'What a Liberty Bill!'
The corner of the wall is painted white because of the blackout. The headlamps of cars were fitted with louvered covers in an attempt to hide them from the air. Consequently they illuminated very little and accidents were all too common after dark. The remnants from the blackout curtains were ingeniously used by the ladies to make skirts and other items of clothing in their 'make do and mend' campaign.

Viewed from the steps of the Walker Art Gallery is the base of the Wellington Memorial. During the war years the Gallery was occupied by the Ministry of Food. Maybe they were the ones responsible for pasting the posters pleading for support for the lads to the base of the column? Everyone was keen to 'do their bit' to bring the war to as speedy a conclusion as possible. They wanted their sons, husbands and fathers home safely. Ration books were accepted a little more willingly. Empty shop windows seemed little to suffer. At home there was a feeling of helplessness. Any opportunity was taken if it would help. When the government introduced conscription to get women to go to work in the factories, on the buses, or to work on the land, they were embarrassingly swamped by eager volunteers. In the distance to the right of the column can be seen the Empire Theatre. It kept open throughout the war and the shows boosted morale. From there many witnessed the flames rising from the roof of St George's Hall, at the other side of Lime Street, when it was hit during an air-raid. They cried at the thought that this architectural gem should be lost. Many of the other buildings seen here did not survive the bombing or the developer's bulldozer. The tram passed the gallery and rattled its way down William Brown Street to Pier Head. It was possible to get there for the princely sum of 2d. The man may be telling the boy that, if he worked hard at school and matriculated (it was not painful to 'matriculate', it simply meant passing your exams!) he too would be able to earn enough to afford a wonderful state-of-the-art motor car like this one, and not have to wait for the tram.

Liverpool Libraries and Information Services

Above: White tablecloths, made whiter with a touch of 'dolly blue', are spread across tables gathered from every home. The precious paper, saved during the years of conflict, has been lavishly folded to make triangular hats. A mother, amongst the parents on the pavement on the left, points at the camera and shouts that mysterious instruction to her child, 'Watch for the birdie'. All of the children show great restraint as they wait for the signal for the feast to begin. Cakes, buns and biscuits have been miraculously conjured up. Every available ration coupon has been generously donated for the VJ day celebrations in Briardale Road, Mossley. Mothers have shown great ingenuity in creating garments from any available pieces of material. They have darned socks, knitted pullovers, revamped 'hand-me-down' clothes, and turned these children out looking neat and tidy. VE day had been celebrated in May of 1945, but for many it had seemed a little premature to celebrate an end to war when their husbands, fathers and sons were still fighting in the Far East. On the 6th August an atom bomb was dropped on Hiroshima. On the 9th August a plutonium bomb was dropped on Nagasaki. New words of horror entered our vocabularies. With the second bomb, one hundred thousand people were killed, and thousands more injured for life. The bomb was dropped from an American Super-fortress named 'Enola Gay' after the captain's mother. Quite whether she would have wanted her name attached to this deliverer of so much death can only be guessed. The Japanese surrendered shortly after.

Bird's eye view

In 1960 Frank Norman and Lionel Bart could well have had Liverpool City centre in mind when they wrote, 'Fings Ain't What They Used To Be'. With the old St John's market demolished, the cranes stand ominously over the Playhouse. Soon a towering, four hundred and fifty foot high, Beacon, will replace them. It will have a restaurant perched on high giving a view, on a good day, from the mountains of Wales to the hills of the Pennines. During the sixties there were other significant changes to Liverpool's skyline. The giant round church, tent-like in shape, capped by a lantern tower, certainly gave everyone a subject for conversation. Some of the descriptions were anything but flattering. The Roman Catholic Cathedral dominated the landscape. It was bold in its concept and affirmed that Christianity is alive and unafraid to assert itself.

The Opera house, used as a cold store, can be clearly seen, is soon to be demolished. In the near foreground, the arch of Lime Street station can just be seen, with the towers on the facade of the Concourse House silhouetted against St George's Place. Beyond Owen and Owen are the buildings of George Henry Lee stores. On the left of the photograph, the curving entrance of the Forum Cinema stands at the top of Elliot Street. Like many others, it fell to the increasing popularity of the television. In the fifties the television had seemed like an amusing novelty for the wealthy, but now it was an essential piece of furniture in every home.

Liverpool Libraries and Information Services

Above: Many sailors from many parts of the world would know immediately where they were if they saw these three monolithic buildings on the shore. They would recognise the 'geese', the liver birds, or more correctly the cormorants roped to their perches, silhouetted against Liverpool's skyline. It was one of the first buildings to be constructed in reinforced concrete, but it was clad in granite.

The architect Arnold Thornley designed the domed building, resembling a palace. It is the offices of the Mersey Docks and Harbour Board. The largest dome was taken from a design by Professor Sir Charles Reilly. It had been submitted in the competition for the Anglican Church in 1902. In the centre is the Cunard Building, which would not be out of place in Venice.

Behind these buildings can be seen the overhead railway. Swept away in the plans for the city development, but it was

beneath. To the right of this can be seen the facade of a building with two towers on the corners. If the reader thinks that it resembles the old Scotland Yard building in London it is not surprising, as the same architect, R Norman Shaw, designed it.

Top: When the Mersey Tunnel opened in 1934 it was the longest underwater highway in the world. From the air it is a thing of beauty, looking remarkably 'modern'. It was considered a marvel of engineering in its time, and indeed, it still is. Cynics said that it was built as much to keep men in work as for any other reason. It is true that National Government, at a time of high unemployment, was encouraging building in all forms. Money was being made available for first time house buyers, and large numbers of council houses were being built.

As the hole was dug the question arose regarding what was to be done with the earth, sand, and rock excavated from it. Liverpool already had a major problem with the disposal of waste, but now there were thousands of tons of spoil. It was decided to tip the material onto marshy ground alongside the Mersey. They levelled it, planted shrubs and created playing fields and parks. This promenade area overlooking the Mersey was then named Otterspool. It was an excellent solution to the problem, as well as providing a resource for which generations to come will thank the planners.

The setting sun is casting long shadows as the trams wend their way up and down Dale Street, and William Brown Street. Shadows of a different kind were being cast over Europe in 1934. The Nazis began the sterilisation of the so-called 'inferior' Germans. More than fifty thousand Jews were sterilised in 1934. They even changed the words of the Psalms to get rid of any reference to the Jews.

considered by some to be a short sighted action as it could have helped to alleviate the pressure on traffic in the city by carrying passengers to new housing areas which developed on the perimeter of the city. Although in need of a major overhaul, with some investment it could possibly have continued to provide a valuable service.

Behind is the white tower of the Mersey Tunnels Offices building, which acts as a ventilation funnel for the tunnel

Above: From high above, we have a spectacular view of the White City Greyhound track in 1932. Perhaps it offered the hope of easy money to people who were still on low wages during the depression of the early thirties. Or perhaps there was further misery, when hard earned money literally 'went to the dogs'. It was a time of contrasts. Some had the cash to buy the newly invented vacuum cleaners and electric ovens now available in the shops. If a couple were earning four hundred pounds a year in 1932, they could afford to buy a car.

This particular day seems like a good one to drive up the quiet A57 past the Stanley Abattoir (just out of the picture beyond the other bowling green), or along Church Road seen at the bottom of our picture.

Beyond the stadium, at the other side of the railway line, is the athletics track and bowling greens, which are still in service today. The greyhound track closed on 6th October 1973, and the nineteen-acre site was used for the markets, which had moved from Queen Square and Cazneau Street. One advantage of the move was the space to park up to seven hundred lorries. The roads would never be so quiet again; this is definitely the right time to own your car!

There were those who preferred to go to the 'flicks' instead of 'the dogs'. They could see the new 'Tarzan the Ape Man', Johnny Weissmuller, or shiver at the performance of Boris Karloff in 'Frankenstein'. The government even allowed the cinemas to open on a Sunday!

Here at Georges 'Lanny' (landing stage) the ferry waits to cross the Liverpool Bay to Birkenhead or Wallasey. It is 1949 and sweets are still rationed! The trams are still running, but there is little shelter for the passengers on a wet and windy day. The trams were often referred to as 'Green Goddesses', and a conductor always accompanied tram and bus drivers at this time. The conductor was better known by some as 'the guard'. His job was to collect the fares and assist in swinging the pantograph, that arm which gathered power from the overhead wire, to face the opposite direction for the return journey. Sparks showered on a frosty morning as the pantograph magnetically snapped the last inches onto the wire. The music hall comedian would say that it was possible to be electrocuted if a person placed one foot on the metal track and touched the overhead wire with his finger. The wheels rumbled on the tracks as the vehicle made its way along. A metal cage almost brushed the ground to safely scoop away anyone who fell in front of the wheels.

On this day in June the weather seems fine and the crossing will be smooth. When the wind blows into the estuary from the sea, and the tide is turning, the journey over the white crests of the waves can be an invigorating experience.

In January 1949 Tommy Handley died. He was famous for his part in the radio programme 'Its That Man Again', which had celebrated its three hundredth performance in October of the previous year.

Liverpool Libraries and Information Services

We can all remember sitting on the old school bench for they were the happiest days of our lives, or so we have been constantly reminded. The former pupils of Gwladys Street School, Walton Road will have their own memories of 1949, just as those of us who are approaching pensionable age or beyond can recall of their formative years. In our schools there often was, first and foremost, the headmistress with her hair in a bun, an avowed man hater who loved nothing better than wielding the cane across the palms of hands belonging to some little lad who had the temerity to tweak some girl's pigtails. Heaven help him if he was unable to recite his seven times table backwards as well because that meant another crack across the knuckles with a 12 inch ruler. Those times in the classroom with an old male teacher, too aged to have been in the war, were just as memorable. He wore a jacket with leather elbow patches and smelt of stale Woodbines as he taught us all about nouns, adjectives and adverbs and made us back our books with brown paper. These were really useful lessons to someone who was going to spend the major portion of his working life operating a crane on the docks. If these were the best days of our lives then adulthood must have been an awful experience.

On the move

Above: The light from an Atlas lamp shone more brightly than the brain of this pedestrian dodging the tram as he nipped across Lord Street. In 1955 he still had a couple more years of death defying road crossing to undertake before the rails were removed and buses gained a monopoly in the city's public transport. Liverpool was still coming to terms with postwar regeneration as bomb sites waited to be cleared completely. New buildings were erected on the waste land created by the enemy bombing of over a decade earlier, but such had been the devastation that it seemed an eternity before all the scars were removed. Some might suggest that a number of the replacement structures were their own blots on the landscape as the fetish for straight lines, concrete and steel seemed to dominate the thoughts of the architects empowered with the responsibility of forging a new face for the city. We had won the war, but at what cost? Economically, we struggled through rationing and austerity whilst, aesthetically, our eyes took a bashing as beauty and grandeur gave way to a culture of utility and practicality. That architectural attitude persisted for years, long after the times of plenty in the 1960s, and it is only in more recent times that planners have given consideration to form as well as substance.

Pictured at the Pierhead the brand spanking new 'Saxonia' was part of Cunard's ocean going passenger liner fleet that had been operating since the company was founded in 1840. This vessel, built in John Brown's shipyard, had only recently been launched and was the second Cunard liner to bear this name. The previous one was built by CS Swan Hunter in 1900 and served the company for 25 years. On 2 September 1954 the new 'Saxonia' was embarking on its maiden voyage across the Atlantic to Quebec and Montreal with a full complement of 1,375 passengers who enjoyed the very latest in comfort that could be provided. In 1957 she moved to the Southampton-Canada route and started to be used for cruising, though modifications were required to help her adapt to this role. The 'Saxonia' was extensively refitted for this purpose in the winter of 1962-63 and painted green like other cruising Cunarders and following the facelift renamed 'Carmania'. From 1963 to 1967 she plied a Rotterdam-Southampton-Canada route and sailed on winter cruises in the Caribbean and on the Mediterranean. Laid up in 1971 due to a staffing dispute between Cunard and the National Union of Seamen, 'Carmania' was sold to Sovtorflot in 1973 and renamed 'Leonid Sobinov'.

Above: It was 14th September 1957 when the final decommissioning of trams in Liverpool took place. Twenty-six trams went into service that morning. Fourteen travelled route 6A, and twelve on route 40. A flag was raised from the depot clock tower as they had left the Edge End Works that morning. After the peak morning period the buses took over. The last tram in service was number 274 on route 40.

When their work was done they assembled in front of the Docks and Harbour building. The service buses departed from Pier Head to allow the trams to take their correct place on the South Loop and approach track. Amongst the important guests were Bessie Braddock MP, and the Lord Mayor of Liverpool.

When the clock on the Liver Building clock struck 6-00 pm, the band played 'Wish Me Luck As You Wave Me Goodbye'. The ships in the river sounded their horns and the trams moved away

in a slow, dignified convoy. They moved slowly through the streets escorted by police motorcycles and surrounded by buses. Number 210 was decorated and led the procession. Number 293, bearing the sign 'The Last Tram', brought up the rear. As they re-entered the depot, the crowds were held back by a police cordon and the band played 'Auld Lang Syne'. People gathered to get a last glimpse of the 'Green Goddesses'. Number 293 was later sold to an American tram museum. Tram number 245 was selected for preservation. The city of Glasgow bought many of them, and some were scrapped.

Far left: It seems strange that we always miss the normally 'everyday' things in our lives when they are to about to go forever. As we look at this picture we regret the passing of the last tram, even though we realised its limitations, compared with the advantages of the bus that was planned to replace it. Even the old red telephone boxes, overhead wires, and cast iron lampposts become dear to us and gain the status of 'collector's items'.

In pristine condition, number 293 has arrived at the docks from Edge End Works with a police escort. Has it rained this morning, or is this the result of tears from the waiting crowd eagerly waiting to say a fond 'goodbye' to 'Liverpool's Last Tram'? It is ready for its long journey to America. It had been bought by the American Seashore Trolley Museum in May 1958, and was shipped to Boston. From there it would be

transported to its final destination at Kennebunkport in Maine, where trams from all over the world were on show.

During the parade, in September 1957, to mark the end of the use of trams in Liverpool, number 293 had travelled on route 6A to Bowring Park. It had held pride of place in the procession. On that day it had carried a sign announcing that the journey was for the privileged 'ticket holders only'.

Top: Esso, the sign of happy motoring or the petrol that put a tiger in your tank, was the stuff that fuelled the cars at Prout's garage. The impressive frontage on Breck Road, Everton advertised the importance of the British car industry in 1960. At this time the motor car was fast becoming an essential possession for the man in the street, rather than the preserve of the middle classes. Family saloons were snapped up as wages grew and unemployment fell in the Macmillan 'never had it so good' era. The Morris Minor is perhaps the most memorable of the vehicles in Prout's showroom and one example is parked at the kerb to the right of the photograph. This is the model on which Alec Issigonis cut his designing teeth. He joined Morris Motors in 1936 as a suspension designer and developed the Morris Minor. A reliable model with excellent steering and cornering qualities, it was the first all British car to pass the 1,000,000 mark in sales and remained in production from 1948 to 1971. Surviving models are still cherished by owners and collectors. After a brief spell elsewhere he returned to what was now the British Motor Corporation. In response to the Suez energy crisis in 1956 and the popularity of Germany's Volkswagen Beetle, he introduced the boxy, inexpensive, fuel-efficient car that was, from 1962, known universally as the 'Mini'. Black was still the predominant colour for British cars, but that was soon to change as the 60s brought a variety of pastel shades. Young people ended the decade driving cars that had been customised with transfers of flowers and psychedelic patterns.

Liverpool Libraries and Information Services

B uses have operated in Liverpool since 1911, although in a very limited way. They formed an insignificant part of the public passenger service, which was a large electric tram network throughout the city. By 1955, however, Liverpool was almost totally served by buses. During the final stages of replacement of the trams in November 1956, fifteen SKB registered buses, of which fleet number 232 operating on route 500, was one, and fifteen VKB registered entered service. They were front engined, Leyland PD2/20 buses, with a sixty-two-seater body. Many of the drivers and conductors, who had served on the trams, were transferred to the buses.

The youth of the day leapt on and off the rear deck with the same easy grace as Douglas Fairbanks, or Burt Lancaster swung into action on the screen. That is, of course, unless the conductor (the 'guard') was present, or an inspector had come aboard to check all the tickets.

You could only smoke on the upper deck, and it was a great place to meet on the last bus home after a night of dancing, or a visit to the pictures. 'High Society' was the film of 1956. It starred Frank Sinatra, Bing Crosby, Louis Armstrong and the amazing Grace Kelly, who married Prince Rainier II of Monaco in the April. All the young men had their hair combed into a DA at the back, and a 'quiff' pulled forward in the style of their hero, Elvis. At the top of the hit parade was his song 'Heartbreak Hotel', and he was 'ever so lonely baby'!

Below: As we look at this picture it comes as no surprise to learn that Liverpool had a major traffic problem in the early sixties. Some of these workers, leaving Napier's factory at the end of the day, will travel on the waiting buses, some in their cars, and some will ride their environmentally friendly, traffic beating, Sturmey Archer three speed gear, bicycles. They will meet workers from other factories, shops and offices. Many of them will be returning to their homes 'over the water' on the Wirral. Then the fun will begin! It will require only one Austin A35, or one of the million Morris Minors that had been produced up to 1961, to have a puncture, or run out of petrol when they have arrived at, or are in the Mersey tunnel, and, gradually, the whole of Liverpool will be paralysed. Some may be thinking that the train could be their best means of escaping the turmoil in the city centre. However, in 1963 a gentleman called Dr Beeching came up with the idea of closing well over a thousand stations throughout Britain, and there was a rumour that one of these might be Liverpool Exchange Station. Perhaps, with a little modernisation, the overhead railway could have served a useful purpose in the sixties and seventies, but this had been demolished in the name of progress.

At this time a man called Graeme Shankland drew up a plan to solve the city's traffic problems. He sensitively preserved the great architectural gems of Liverpool, and protected the narrow lanes, which are so full of character and history, whilst his plan went a long way towards easing traffic congestion. Many of his ideas were adopted, but with some modifications made.

Liverpool Libraries and Information Services

What a stylish hat, worn by the lady on the right, with a coat with military style buttons, and ankle strap shoes. Few people, ladies or gentlemen, ventured out without some form of headwear. Now that, for the first time since 1941, clothes were no longer rationed, this lady seems determined to raise standards. She strolls along Church Street in 1949 ready to pose for the camera.

For the children of Britain the fact that sweets were no longer rationed was even better news. The dentist's prayer for more cavities had been answered! If the government got its way sugar would soon be nationalised.

The street is thronging with shoppers outside Wynn's and Marks & Spencer's. What would they have thought of a shop with a strange name like 'Next' moving into this neighbourhood? Pedestrians have to dodge the traffic, whilst underfoot the cobblestones have been exposed making walking more difficult. The tramlines create a further hazard for both the pedestrians and the driver of the car whose wheels are in the groove. If they can wait until the early sixties, a town planner called Mr Graeme Shankland will turn the street into a precinct free of all traffic so that they can shop in safety. Until then they will have to go on wondering if the traffic in London really did stop at the beginning of the radio programme 'In Town Tonight'.

Shopping spree

Below: There is little interest shown in the bargains to be had in the sale at Leslies Furs in Great Charlotte Street. The weather was poor, and so were many of the people in 1937. For a family, like the one in the picture, with two children, it was estimated that they would require six pounds per week in order to live reasonably well. The average wage, however, was a little more than two pounds per week, and that assumes that there was work to be found. There may be some who remember Lewis's building before it was destroyed by bombs during the blitz of May 1941.

The coal man manoeuvres his lorry full of coal between pedestrians and a cyclist. Each of them looks as though they have deliveries to make. Perhaps the cyclist is the butcher's 'lad'. When the basket was full the bike was difficult to balance, even when the cobblestones were dry. They had a way of splitting a canvas coal sack along one side, then, having folded one edge back they wore it on their heads like a monk's cowl to protect their necks and backs from the lumpy sacks. The coal men would drop the delivery through the hole in the pavement outside the house directly into the cellar. Lighting a fire was an essential art. The skill of splitting wood with an axe was learnt early in life. The house was bitterly cold until a fire crackled in the grate. There was no central heating in most houses in these days.

Above: Crossings, marked out with studs and the familiar yellow beacon, had been about for a number of years, thirteen to be precise, when these shoppers took advantage of them to get across Church Street. Beacons, such as this one, were made of glass and offered good targets for little vandals with catapults. They gained their stripes and the name 'zebra' in 1951. It was 1952 before they were made of plastic and started winking to make their presence known. In the future they would not be needed as this area became 'pedestrianised', a word not in the vocabulary of these shoppers in 1947.

The motorcyclist, rounding the corner into Basnett Street, need only wear a crash helmet if he so chooses. It would have been more likely that he would wear a flat cloth cap, often back-to-front. With no suspension of any kind at the back of his machine, and only girder fork s at the front, his progress over the cobblestones would have been anything other than smooth. The road would have been clean had he fallen off. The road sweeper has just finished his work and parked dustcart by the kerb. Such workers and their handcarts were once a common sight.

On the right hand corner was Bon Marché, and on the left is Swears and Wells the furriers. Close to where the beacon stands there is now a statue of Sir John Moores and his brother. Sir John was given the freedom of the city at the same time as Bessie Braddock. He was the chairman of Everton FC, and a great promoter of the arts.

Shoppers stroll in the summer sun on this July day in 1947 after one of the worst winters in living memory. The people lived through temperatures of minus twenty-six degrees centigrade. They were not only cold, but often hungry. Although the war had been over for almost two years, rationing was increased. In January many factories had to close their doors because there was not enough coal to keep them going. On the first day of this year the mines were nationalised and plans were laid to increase production. The wintry conditions lasted well into March and an order was made banning coal and gas fires until autumn. It was a case of donning an extra vest and another homemade jumper. 'Work or want' was the government's slogan as the people strived to increase productivity.

The number of cars parked on the cleared bombsite in Church Street seems to give a lie to the petrol shortage. Not a single parking meter in sight, and no risk of being clamped either. Traffic wardens have not yet been invented so let's make the most of the opportunity.

Beneath the magnificent facade of this beautiful building, once the Compton Hotel, Saxone shoe shop is open for business, assuming that you have the clothing coupons and they have any shoes to buy. It was possible to rest your aching feet after shopping and watch the world go past the window of Maison Lyons Café next door. Marks and Spencer's could always be relied on to find something to please the ladies, and there was little risk of animal rights activists storming the corner doorway of Swears and Wells furriers.

Liverpool Libraries and Information Services

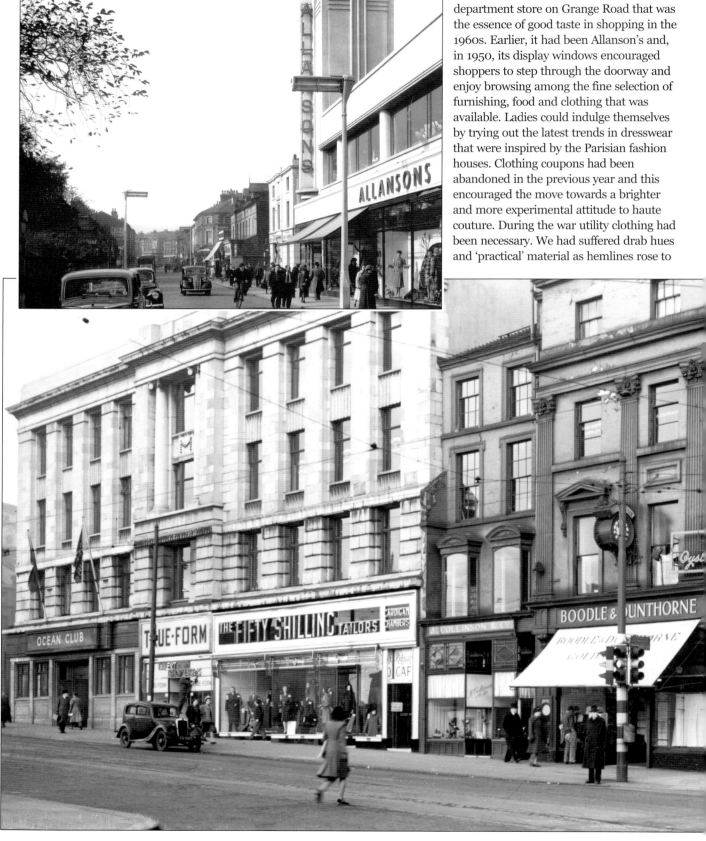

Left: Birkenhead's Beattie's was an elegant department store on Grange Road that was the essence of good taste in shopping in the 1960s. Earlier, it had been Allanson's and, in 1950, its display windows encouraged shoppers to step through the doorway and enjoy browsing among the fine selection of furnishing, food and clothing that was available. Ladies could indulge themselves by trying out the latest trends in dresswear that were inspired by the Parisian fashion houses. Clothing coupons had been abandoned in the previous year and this encouraged the move towards a brighter and more experimental attitude to haute couture. During the war utility clothing had been necessary. We had suffered drab hues and 'practical' material as hemlines rose to conserve cloth. When Christian Dior launched his sensational New Look in 1947, giving women back an hour glass shape, soft shoulders and full billowing skirts, it was a dream come true. The style filtered through to our High Street shops and gave us back our femininity. Harold Wilson, then a junior trade minister, condemned it all as mere frivolity, but what did a mere man know? How could a pipe smoking politician appreciate what it meant to have a skirt that helped a girl sweep into a room in a flounce of velvet and rayon?

Below left: Where the Fifty Shilling Tailors once traded, it is now possible to buy half-price jewellery, a sandwich from the sandwich shop, or a Chinese meal from the restaurant above. In days gone by fifty shillings was the equivalent of two pounds and fifty new pence. For that amount a serviceman, demobbed (demobilised) from the army, was able to purchase a three-piece suit, jacket, waistcoat and trousers. The shops were later taken over by John Colliers. Everyone of a certain age will now be humming the advertising jingle that ended with the words, 'the window to watch'. Next door is the Ocean Club, now occupied by the Nationwide Building Society, is flying flags from the windows. It echoes a time when Liverpool was a great and thriving port. There was a day when there were so many sailors looking for accommodation

ashore, and there were not enough decent places. A group of ship owners and merchants decided to build a sailors' home in Canning Place. It closed its doors for the last time in 1969 and was demolished in 1974.

Boodle and Dunthorne's shop on the corner is still operating, but the traffic lights are not. They are no longer needed as traffic is restricted from this pedestrianised area and trams have been relegated to the museum. This piece of Liverpool has changed only superficially over the years.

Bottom: It is Wednesday the first of October 1947, and the weather is sunny enough for the shops to find it necessary to lower the blinds. The shoppers, who search for the bargains, may call and purchase extra warm undergarments from Hyam's, or woollies from the Scotch Wool and Hosiery Stores, just in case next winter is as severe as the last. Money is tight and rationing has been increased because of the austerity of the time. But this does not prevent the search for a bargain. Wherever a queue formed others joined it and asked what they were queuing for after they had secured their place in it. After all, they would argue, who knows what may have returned to the shelves? They may be able to return home with a rare treat. Many children born before and during the war would now be seven or eight years old and not know what a banana looked like. It was described to them by grandmother and was as rare as the unicorn in her fairy stories. There were many who were disappointed when they first tasted one. They found the texture and taste to be something that had to be acquired. Army vehicles continued to be a common sight well into the fifties. Not all of them belonged to the army any more. Lorries, jeeps and motorcycles could be purchased from the government surplus stock for general use.

Trams are still in use in Liverpool, as in many other parts of the country. They seem a little outdated at a time when the sound barrier was broken.

Liverpool Libraries and Information Services

Below: Cooper's Buildings can be seen beyond the cars, parked on the cleared bombsite. Little do they realise that they are on the spot where the Americans will land! Only in the previous year, 1948, the first McDonald's Hamburger bar had opened in San Bernadino, California. No one knew then that they would spread and one day occupy this place in Liverpool. Trams are still in service to and fro on Lord Street, and another route follows across Paradise Street. Bunney's and other shops have lowered their blinds to protect the goods in their windows and offer some protection from the weather, although it does not seem very sunny on this day in May 1949. On 9th January of this year, Tommy Handley died. He was famous for his part in the radio show, 'It's That Man Again'. The show was affectionately called 'ITMA'. Born in Liverpool, Tommy Handley was only one of the many comedians to come from the city. Arthur Askey, Rob Wilton, Ted Ray, Jimmy Tarbuck and, of course, Ken Dodd, who claimed that jam butties were mined at Knotty Ash. Like Ken, Tommy used the names of people, places, and words that he remembered from his hometown, and the days of his youth. Tommy Handley used the word 'Scousers' to describe Liverpudlians, and 'scouse' to mean the dialect spoken by them. Before ITMA 'scouse' generally meant a meat stew. Maybe the ladies are on their way home with some cheap cuts of mutton in their baskets to make a 'scouse' stew.

Right: Lots of goods on sale here in St John's market in 1951. The banners are flying. It is Festival of Britain week. On the South Bank of the Thames, a large bombsite was chosen as the place where the Great Exhibition of 1851 would be commemorated. But it was to be more than that. It was to be a fling to end the years of austerity and celebrate British achievement. It was to herald the start of new prosperity. The shape of the future rose in the middle of the exhibition in the form of a giant dome, with a diameter of three hundred and sixty five feet. If this sounds familiar it may be because the minister in charge of the exhibition was Herbert Morrison. He was the grandfather of Peter Mandelson, who used the idea again for the millennium dome. Children, who were unable to go to the exhibition, could buy paper models to build. They had all seen it on Movie-tone Newsreels. Everyone could recognise the Skylon, that cigar shaped sculpture was suspended above the exhibition. Some considered the plan to be an irresponsible waste of money. But to the surprise of the critics it turned out to be a considerable success as it caught the imagination of many people. It did much to restore morale after the years of austerity. So, people of Liverpool, pose for the camera and enjoy the fact that things are slowly returning to 'normal'. We must ask the question, 'Who is that smart chap with the bow tie and trilby hat'?

Although the Beatles have made Italian suits, narrow ties, and long hair, into the popular garb of the day, mum still thought it was healthy to wear short trousers and socks. 'Twelve was soon enough to be dressed like a man. No point growing up before your time. Get a bit of fresh air around your legs.' School uniform dictated the same in those days.

Few ventured out without a hat in 1963. Headscarves, in printed silk, were the popular wear for the ladies. They were so convenient as they could be folded and fit into the corner of a handbag. They were practical even if they were not glamorous and, after all, not everyone can look like Elizabeth Taylor. She had appeared on screen in the most revealing outfits in the new film, 'Cleopatra'. The Queen wore a headscarf so it was certainly good enough for the rest of us.

There is now plenty on sale in the brightly lit shops in St John's Market. All good British produce. Meat cut to your liking and weighed out in front of the customer. Sausages were cut from a long string. No pre-packaging here. The eggs had a little lion stamped on them guaranteeing freshness. We were advised to 'go to work on an egg'. (The lion was removed from eggs in 1968). Soon we would all be shopping at the supermarkets that were gradually establishing themselves, and the town planners would have their eye on St John's Market.

Above: The year is 1963 and there were some world-shaking events, one of which was the assassination of John F Kennedy, the president of the USA. Some lads from Liverpool, who sported mop-top haircuts, topped the charts with songs like 'Please Please Me', 'She Loves You', 'From Me To You', and a string of others. They shook the pop world, and were invited to appear on the Royal Variety Performance. Henry Cooper suffered several serious blows at the hands of an amazing talent in the boxing ring. He was Cassius Clay, later to change his religion, and his name to become known as Mohammed Ali.

St John's Market was also soon to be dealt a devastating blow as it fell to the developer's bulldozer. Liverpool is blessed with fine, monolithic buildings, but there was still some regret when it was demolished.

If you went late on a Saturday there was always a bargain to be had. Stallholders didn't want to be left with anything perishable. After all, deep freezers, and even fridges, were still a luxury item in most homes. Some houses had a stone cellar, where things could be kept cool so that they would last longer. It was usual to shop more frequently and buy fresh food. Weren't we all suspicious of the idea of freezing things for any length of time? It couldn't be right. It wasn't natural.

We liked to know that things were solid and reliable - our buildings and entrances were held up with columns that could be relied on, and made to last a hundred years nor more. Post boxes were made of cast-iron, painted bright red so that they could be seen. 'Royal' mail - definitely not to be messed with! That would surely never change!

Left: Market Street echoes with the cries of vendors competing for attention, each with their own witty line in patter. They could charm the last few pennies from the purses of the people gathered around. They could bring a smile to their faces with jokes about current affairs, and they had plenty of ammunition in 1963. The Tory minister John Profumo had lied about knowing the notorious Christine Keeler. There was a scandal. The newspapers and the music hall comedians had a 'field day'. There were no jokes made about the other big story of the year, however - this being the assassination of the American President. Maybe this rug is just the thing to replace that old one that we had made ourselves from strips of cloth threaded through the weave of a piece of canvas. We were proud of it when it was first made, but it has a few burns in it now, caused by sparks from the fire. It took the children hours to tear the strips of cloth and cut

then to the right length. Mother and Granny had woven them into a simple pattern. Would we dare to call out the moment they announce the amazing price for this bargain? Tension is building as this treasure is described to the waiting crowd. The only way that some of the poor people in this crowd would be able to buy things on impulse would be if they robbed a train, but that had already been done. The Great Train Robbery took place in 1963, when a Post Office train was stopped and robbed of two and a half million pounds.

Below left: The ladies, in 1963, must have rebelled. There are very few of them in Upper Dawson Street market on this day. The men must have been sent out to see if they could make the four pounds housekeeping go further. There is certainly a lot of interest at the handbag stall - surely Liverpool men have not undergone such a change in 1963? Could it be the music being played which is having an effect on them? Cliff Richard and Elvis Presley are still dominating the pop scene with their wholesome music. Elvis hairstyles are much in evidence. Mothers covered the backs of the chars and

settees with an antimacassar to protect the fabric from Brylcreem. In the south of England the fashion was for Rhythm and Blues, whilst in the north 'rock and roll' was still favourite. The press hardly noticed a new Liverpool group when they published their first record in October 1962. The song was 'Love Me Do'. In January 1962, Decca records made a little mistake when they refused them a contract because they didn't think they would 'make it'. But between 1963 and 1966 everyone took notice

as the group had eleven number one hit singles! It may have been a tough fight to get through the crowd in the market, but nowhere near as tough as the fight Henry Cooper had with a bragging boxer called Cassius Clay. He 'floated like a butterfly' and certainly 'stung like a bee'. Elizabeth Taylor was in the audience and, like many others, she shouted for the referee to stop the fight. Tommy Little, the referee, responded and stopped the punishment Henry was receiving.

Bottom: There is great interest in the goods on sale in the temporary market set up in Clayton Square, and a large crowd is gathering. Maybe there is a trader shouting to gather them around as he tells them that the only way to get meat cheaper than his is to steal it from the back of a lorry! The exciting prospect even attracts a few male shoppers, a rare thing in the fifties, unless they were elderly pensioners. The men of the day thought shopping to be a woman's work. The ladies, however, had experienced the responsibility of work; they had kept the wheels of industry turning during the recent war, and now they were agitating for change. Despite adverts all around them featuring pictures of smiling, well manicured middle-class housewives going about their daily chores pushing a vacuum cleaner that 'beats as it sweeps as it cleans', there was a restlessness and a desire for equality. Maybe, though, they will call at Lewis's after the open market just to see what new gadgets are on offer to releases them from the drudgery of house work. There may be some of those 'trannies' (transistor radios) - they can be taken anywhere, they are told. They operate from batteries. You could listen to Lady Isobel Barnett guessing the occupation of the contestants in 'What's My Line?' whilst you were in the kitchen. What will they think of next? Does anyone remember those shopping bags with a red tartan pattern printed into the leatherette material from which they were made?

Liverpool Libraries and Information Services

The Americans came over here in their countless thousands during the war and their influence remained long after Burtonwood fell into disrepair. They left behind their chewing gum, jitterbug dancing, nylon stockings and a memory of brash and flash youth to go with a number of broken hearts that littered Merseyside. Even our language was affected as young people aped the expressions that they had heard the GIs use. 'Sure', 'Yeah' and 'OK' became commonplace ways of saying roughly the same thing that 'yes' meant to the rest of the population. The American culture even permeated the playthings that our children used to pass away their leisure hours. Once they had been satisfied with any old toy car or soapbox, but now it had to be a jeep, one of the General Purpose or GP vehicles that our transatlantic cousins used so regularly. This 1947 photograph shows that the models had to be truly authentic to satisfy demand, right down to the single star painted on the bonnet, or should that be 'hood'? As the assembly line workers churned out the replicas they must have wondered what future peacetime held for them as the country tried to get back onto its feet after six years of deprivation and devastation. The world that they had left behind at the end of the 1930s had changed forever. Britain was having to come to terms with the realisation that it was no longer a super power. The Empire was crumbling and we were having to look across the 'big pond' for both a lead in policy and a handout in economic aid.

Making a living

Below: Working away, like little beavers, these men are not building a dam to block the canal, but the leaning timber frame looks very unsafe. The chairs may give a clue as to their purpose. Chairs are being fixed to this Heath Robinson structure. They don't really expect anyone to risk life and limb by sitting on them, or do they? The canal runs close to, and parallel with, the straight stretch of the track at Aintree affording an excellent view of the racing. Maybe some Grand National enthusiasts, in 1938, may take a gamble in order to have this grandstand view of the race. Possibly the added danger and the exciting events on the track may take their minds from the possibility of a world war. Neville Chamberlain had received a note from Hitler, and declared that it was, 'peace for our time'. The next day the Germans had marched into Poland unopposed. William Lynn, the landlord of the Waterloo Hotel in Ranelagh Street, was famed locally as a great fryer of fish, but he was a character who also had a love of sport. He sponsored a hare-coursing event and named it 'the Waterloo Cup'. Later he turned to horse racing and leased some land at Aintree. In 1829 Lord Molyneux laid the foundation stone, and, according to some, buried a bottle full of sovereigns inside the footings. The meeting, in October of that year, was a flat race over one and a quarter miles, called the Croxteth Stakes. A horse called 'Mufti' won it.

Right: They might have been at the Cammell Laird shipyard, but these white collar workers had never wielded an acetylene torch or spanner in their lives. From the look of their bowler hats, brief cases and hankies in their breast pockets it was not so much anchor chains but the chain of command that interested them. The man gazing aloft has made the remarkable discovery that the large container towering above him is something that people call a ship. Cammell Laird had a few of them in 1961. It was as far back as the 1820s when the birth of the renowned shipbuilding tradition came into being as William Laird opened his shipyard. This inspired a host of other port-related industries to come into existence, such as flour milling, tanning, edible oil refining and the manufacture of paint and rubber-based products. He also laid out the nucleus of the town of Birkenhead on a grid plan. Laird's combined with Cammell's shipbuilding company in 1903 to form the famous name that was to the forefront of the industry during the first threequarters of the 20th century. The docks that had seen such famous ships as Achilles (1931), Ark Royal (1937), Prince of Wales (1939) and Thetis (1939) sail out of the Cammell Laird shipyards was still a busy place as these men held their meeting. Yet, by the 1970s the dockland was a sadder place as shipping declined and yards closed.

Below: This photograph, taken at the docks in 1957, should carry a government health warning, not for the activity taking place but for those sufferers from vertigo now looking at the picture. A queasy stomach and goosebumps on the back of the neck will be part of the experiences some readers might be going through at this very moment. Perched many feet in the air, this pair of intrepid workers must have had a real head for heights as they toiled away, oblivious to the precarious nature of their perches. They were answering one of those questions that are like the ones about the chicken and the egg or flies and winter. If you need a crane to build structures, how do you erect the crane in the first place? This is just what they were doing and the cables and pulleys upon which they relied to swing girders into place required their personal touch to guide them exactly into the right spot. To these workers there was nothing unusual about their job. After all, had they not trained on Meccano as children? This was just an example of putting into practice the skills they had learned from bolting together Frank Hornby's imaginative toy when they were youngsters.

A number of vessels had borne the name 'Windsor Castle' and this was the latest of them under construction in 1957. Built by Cammell Laird at Birkenhead, this member of the Union Castle line was powered by twin screw Pametrada geared turbine engines capable of producing a speed of over 22 knots. This mighty passenger liner required 475 crew to service its many needs and provide a delightful experience for the 191 first class and 591 tourist passengers. Queen Elizabeth, the Queen Mother, launched the 'Windsor Castle' on 23 June 1959 in a greatly publicised ceremony that was covered live on the BBC television network. A severe nosebleed threatened to delay the event, but the calm Queen Mum took control and carried out the christening only a minute past its scheduled time of 1:30 pm. That was a typically stoic attitude towards a sense of duty that helped endear her to the nation and on into the 21st century until her sad passing in 2002. At the time of the ship's launch she was the largest liner built in England, the largest owned by Union Castle and the first Union Castle liner constructed at Cammell Laird. Her maiden voyage from Southampton to Durban began on 18 August 1960 and was completed in just over 11 days. The great vessel was the flagship of the Union Castle fleet, but sadly her career was shortlived. She was taken out of service in 1977 and sold to John S. Latsis, the Greek oil and shipping tycoon.

Above: Loading lampshades onto an army lorry in 1947 was obviously a job that took many hands to carry out, or was it that these young women on Buchanan Street took the opportunity to exchange banter with the lads in uniform? The events of that summer gave them plenty to talk about for it was a period of contrasting doom and gaiety. On the one hand there was the economic crisis that led to American aid being sought under the Marshall Plan, food rations being cut and government slogans such as 'Work or Want' and 'Export or Die', and yet we had other things to cheer about. Denis Compton, the original Brylcreem boy, was smashing records and the ball all over the cricket field, Christian Dior was revolutionising women's fashion and Princess Elizabeth announced her engagement to Philip Mountbatten. The young people in the photograph definitely looked on the bright side of life if their smiling faces are a true reflection of their characters, but there were dire warnings coming from church leaders of the dangers of dalliance with the opposite sex. The Bishop of Willesden said that temptation was rife in offices, shops and factories and warned young school leavers of the pressure and strain they would be under in the workplace. Whilst it was true that the divorce rate had shot up, the Bishop was hardly likely to stop innocent flirting that had been going on since Eve was a lass.

There is nothing quite so colourful and exciting as the sights, smells, and sounds of a bustling market, be it an open market in Queen Square or a wholesale fish market like this one. The bidding and bartering are over for the day at Great Charlotte Street in 1963. Now it is the work of clearing the debris ready for another busy day. Soon it would be moved to the site adjacent to the Stanley Abattoir, just as the markets in Queen Square, and Cazneau Street had been moved to the site opposite, between Prescot Road and Edge Lane. Modern, warm, covered markets are wonderful, but something has been lost, we feel, when we look back and remember the open markets. The narrow streets and alleyways, such as Hackins Hey and Leather Lane, were filled with the cries of flower sellers and barrow boys. Handcarts, like the one in the picture, would be wheeled onto their pitch and their merchandise displayed. They were colourful bazaars where a second-hand bargain could be found. Could it just be the passing of time, and the songs the Spinners sang about 'Liverpool Barrer Boy' that makes us feel this way? After all it was a hard way to earn a living.

The flower sellers and barrow boys were well known characters in the city, but the decision was made to 'move them along' Before they were completely washed away in the tide of progress they made a final protest to parliament with a petition signed by, literally, thousands of supporters, but to no avail. Like the Great Charlotte Street wholesale market they exist only in the memory.

Delicate work was required at the Hornby factory on Binns Road. The finishing touches to the hand painted models of sports cars, buses and locomotives had to be just so, otherwise some little boy would not have appreciated his 1957 Christmas present. What fun lads had with the products that had been turned out for over half a century, allowing them to use their imaginations with Grand Prix contests they organised on the living room floor with the toy racing cars they collected. They whizzed them underneath bridges made out of Meccano and transported them out into the hallway on the backs of wagons pulled along tracks laid for their Dublo locomotives. That was if dad could be persuaded to stop fiddling with the transformer and just let his son get on with playing with what were, after all, his toys. The Hornby name was born in 1901 when Frank Hornby (1863-1936) formed Meccano Ltd to make construction toys. In 1920 the company developed the first Hornby train which was produced in metal and powered by clockwork. They were an instant success due to their solid quality and in 1925 the first electric train was produced. In 1964 the model railway manufacturers were experiencing a severe recession and this led to the take over of Meccano by Lines Bros who merged their own Tri-ang Railways and the Meccano Hornby range to rename it Tri-ang Hornby. The Tri-ang Group itself was sold in 1971 and the model railway system regained its name as Hornby Railways.

Heads peeking over the wall demonstrate what an inquisitive strain the human race has in its makeup, especially when trouble is afoot or disaster strikes. However, the dedicated firefighters had no interest in being the centre of attention for they had a job to do, and a dangerous one at that. This warehouse fire in 1961 was straining their talents to the limits and drawing on all the expertise that they had obtained as the result of hours of training and drill. Not only had they to contend with the potential of falling masonry, there was always the possibility of toxic substances within the walls that they were hosing down. Modern firefighting is a far cry from those Victorian days when, in 1843, an Act of Parliament allowed the council to use water from the Mersey for street cleaning, sewer flushing and tackling fires. Indeed, a well in Green Lane was sunk in 1846 specifically for fire fighting. In the early days fire brigades were often the responsibility of insurance companies anxious to protect themselves from the increasing cost of expensive payouts to factory owners and private individuals living and working in more and more overcrowded conditions as the industrial revolution approached its peak. These privately run brigades were gradually taken over by councils and corporations keen to regularise health and safety arrangements.

Branching out over two centuries

Today the name of builders, plumbers and timber merchants Beesley & Fildes Ltd is amongst the best known in the region. But that position of eminence was not acquired overnight. It has taken nearly two hundred years of effort by the Beesley family to turn a once small family firm into the large enterprise it has become.

In the early 1800s it was common practice for a son to follow his father's footsteps as his chosen profession. But this was not the case for 21 year old Robert Beesley: and what made Robert's decision even more unusual was that his ancestors were professional ale tasters!

Robert's father and grandfather were paid by the local parish to taste and test the ale in public houses around the parish to ensure that the local brews were up to scratch.

Robert Beesley however decided that a beer taster's life was not for him

and in the 1820s set himself up as a master painter, plumber and glazier with a shop at 39 Eccleston Street in Prescot.

In 1841 Robert Beesley was joined by his son James. In the 1851 census Robert is recorded as employing six men at his premises. In the following years father and son continued to build a sound family business until 1859 when Robert passed away.

James Beesley continued where his father left off. In the quaint language of the period an advert in the Prescot Reporter for January 1870 placed by James read 'In thanking the gentry and the general public for their past favours, again begs to remind them of his large stock of paper hangings which will be found complete and comprises hanging of every description and quality. Water closets gas fitting executed'.

In 1871 after operating from the same premises for almost 50 years James decided to move the business to larger premises at 26 Eccleston Street just along the road. There the extra space allowed James to expand his

Top: Founder Robert Beesley. **Above left:** *James Beesley, son of the founder.* **Left:** *William Beesley's shop in Aspinal Street, Prescot, 1902. William can be seen in the hat looking out of the window with his two sons at his side, and his wife in the far window.* **Below:** *William Beesley (son of James).*

range and to sell goods to other tradesmen in the area to whom he was soon offering baths, water closets, pumps, gas fittings, lead pipes and wall paper.

By 1881 James employed 11 men and 7 boys. And if trade was slack, as it often was in the winter, James kept his joiners busy in the quiet months making coffins for local undertakers

On his death in 1887 James passed the running of the business over to two of his sons, Joseph and William.

The partnership between the two brothers however did not last very long - a mere 15 months. In 1890, after the break up, William continued to work in the trade though from new premises at Park Mount, Aspinal Street in Prescot.

William Beesley was another master plumber and decorator and he continued to contract for work and to sell products from his shop. William successfully ran the family business until he was forced to retire due to ill health in 1919, though he was to live until 1950, and the firm passed to his son.

After the first world war William's son William-Joseph who had been injured while on service in France asked his brother-in-law, expert craftsman and grainer James Fildes, to join the business. The pair agreed to pool their war gratuity money to expand the business and as a result the Beesley & Fildes name came in to being. James Fildes however withdrew his money out of the partnership after only a few weeks

because he thought the venture too risky; despite that the firm still retained its new name.

In fact James Fildes even stayed with the firm and saw it flourish; he worked as head foreman and many examples of his fine timber graining and marbling can still be seen around Prescot and the surrounding areas - one being the benches in Prescot Parish Church.

By the 1920s the business had moved to new locations: Houghton Street, and to Scotchbarn Lane, Prescot where a branch still remains.

William-Joseph's sons Jack and Bill joined the family business in 1947. A decision was made to promote the retail side of the business via a shop in Chapel Street, Prescot selling wallpaper and paints. Father and sons continued to work together until 1956 when William-Joseph retired.

In 1960, two years after William-Joseph's death, the character of the business changed following a decision taken by Jack to concentrate entirely on the retail side of the business and to stop providing contracting services.

Top left: William Joseph Beesley (son of William). *Above:* Invoices from 1907 (right) and 1965. *Right:* Jack Beesley (son of William J Beesley). *Below left:* Beesley and Fildes timber warehouse. *Below:* In the building yard.

extensive refit and development was then carried out at the branches in Birkenhead, Prestatyn and Chester. The year 2000 saw the opening of a new dedicated plumbers and tile merchants and bathroom showroom in Grafton Street, Liverpool importing tiles directly from manufacturers in Spain and Italy.

In the early 1980s Bill retired and Jack Beesley was in turn joined by his sons John, Paul and Gerard and in 1987 the family expanded the business by opening a new yard in Huyton. Jack Beesley would retire in 1988 after 43 years in the business leaving the firm in the capable hands of the three sons.

Now the business was driven rapidly forward with a purpose built timber yard being opened in 1989, Chattles Timber Importers was acquired and in 1994 a new purpose built timber mill was built in Huyton to enable the company to satisfy the ever growing timber market. New yards were acquired in Liverpool in 1995, Birkenhead in 1997 and Chester and Prestatyn in 1999. An

The development and expansion programme of the business would continue with an old cinema and land adjacent to the Birkenhead site being bought in 1999 with demolition work soon underway to develop the yard at that branch.

In 2001 Beesley & Fildes would also open its HSS Agency Hire Shop at its Huyton and Prestatyn branches whilst the following year a new roofing centre would open on land bought for that purpose in Huyton.

Back in the 1820s when the young Robert Beesley decided to give ale tasting a miss and set up on his own he could never have guessed or anticipated that the firm he founded, passed down from father to son through the generations, would still be going strong at the start of the third millennium.

Top right: *Paul, John and Gerard Beesley.* **Top left, and bottom:** *The company's sites in Prestatyn (top left) Chester (top left, inset) and Grafton Street, Liverpool 8 (bottom).* **Left:** *John Beesley, Managing Director of Beesley & Fildes Ltd, Wilson Road, Huyton.*

Taking one's medicine

From humble beginnings as a sole chemist running a druggist's shop in Worcester, GlaxoSmithKline's Speke site would become part of a world leading pharmaceutical organisation employing over 100,000 people worldwide.

In the early 1800s when John Evans started in business the method of drug making was very crude: raw materials were herbs, minerals and animal products which were formed into tinctures, poultices, soups and teas. It was said that the only difference then between a medicine and a poison was the dose! The majority of drugs were prescribed, prepared and dispensed by physicians. As the workload increased, and the science more demanding, doctors delegated the dispensing to assistants called apothecaries who soon became independent and set up shops of their own. As awareness and training developed dispensing

increasingly became the responsibility of these newly trained pharmacists.

John Evans was born in 1787. By 1809 he was trading as a druggist in Worcester; nine years later this shop was being run by John's brother Edward (later appointed chemist to the King), whilst John became a partner in the firm of Kempson Yates, Evans and Parkinson a large London based firm of wholesale druggists. This venture was soon followed in 1821 by another partnership Stable, Evans and Co which was to be dissolved in 1823.

Top left: Founder, John Evans. *Above:* 'Worcester Gout Medicine', prepared by Edward Evans whilst in partnership with his brother, John, from 1809 - 1818. *Right:* Edward Evans, brother of the founder.
Below: Evans Sons & Co, Hanover Street, 1848.

It was not to be until 1828 that a long term partnership emerged this time with Joseph Sidney Lescher to create the firm of Evans & Lescher.

Joseph Lescher established the Liverpool branch of the business in 1833 along with John Evan's three sons: Thomas, John Hilditch and Edward Evans.

By 1835 John Hilditch Evans was left in charge of the Liverpool business which in 1840 would be renamed Evans Sons & Co.

Drug mills and laboratories were opened in Liverpool's Fleet Street in 1846, a year after Edward Evans had taken charge. Business in Liverpool was booming and in 1848 the Company took over the former Bank of England premises in Hanover Street.

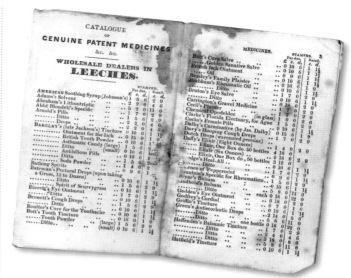

By the mid 1800s the Company had evolved into a successful business with manufacturing and mill facilities in London and Liverpool. Liverpool was selected as a Northern base because of its proximity to the docks and the availability of the raw materials which arrived there from around the world. Technology was now entering the pharmaceutical world in the form of pill and potion making which transferred much of the work away from the pharmacist, whilst with the publication of the first modern British Pharmacopeia in 1864 more control was introduced into pharmaceutical manufacture.

Company founder John Evans died in 1865. Two years later a major fire destroyed a large part of the premises in Hanover Street; as a result of the fire, orders would be temporarily supplied from London until the factory could be rebuilt to modern specifications and to become the Company Head office.

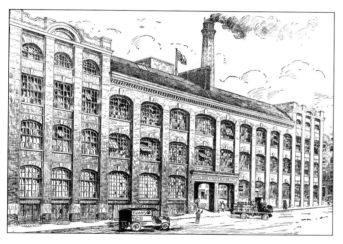

Towards the end of the 19th century, shop fittings became part of the Evans' business with a special part of the Liverpool factory set aside specially for the fitting out of chemist shops.

It was however the manufacture of pharmaceuticals which would continue as the core of the business. The last years of the 19th century and the opening ones of

Top left: Joseph Sydney Lescher, long term business partner of John Evans. *Top right:* A catalogue of medicines owned by John Evans. *Above left:* Drug mills and laboratories opened in Fleet Street in 1846. *Left:* An 1850s Montserrat Lime Juice van.

the 20th century were to become a legendary era for the pharmaceutical industry. An explosion of new scientific discoveries began in Germany with the launch of such things as aspirin, and Salvarsan, the original 'Magic Bullet' and the world's first modern drug.

In 1904 new labs were built in Fleet Street; all 'galenicals' (drugs made from plant extracts rather than chemicals) were now manufactured here along with pills and tablets. Drug milling was carried out and the first vacuum plants for preparing tinctures and liquid extract of cascara and liquorice installed. A most important part of the work was Counter Adjuncts - the forerunner of today's generic or un-branded products.

New premises were built in Seel Street in 1913; a five storey building designed and built by Sir Aston Webb, the famous architect who helped design Buckingham Palace. It was joined to the Hanover Street building by a link bridge and would offer state of the art facilities, including being lit by electricity throughout.

When the founder's son John James Evans died in 1917 it would herald rapid change; Edward Evans became Chairman but ten weeks later died unexpectedly and William Patterson Evans followed him - though he would himself only hold the post for five years leading to the appointment of James Herbert E Evans.

It was a difficult time for both owners and employees alike, as the economy of the country was not doing well. In 1921 the Company agreed with staff to pay reduced wages, though by 1929 things had improved sufficiently for the business to be able to grant workers with fewer than ten years service an annual one week's paid holiday and those with more than 10 years service 10 days holiday.

The start of the first world war in 1914 caused many problems for the Company, not only did more than 400 employees eventually leave to join the armed forces but high prices were coupled with shortages. The high cost of freight more than doubled the cost of goods: synthetic chemicals (which had previously been imported from Germany), essential oils from France, olive oil from Italy and oil of lemon from Sicily were all particularly affected.

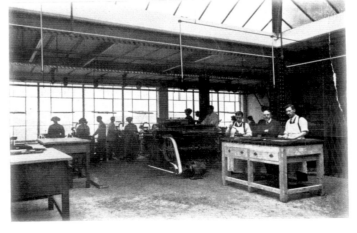

At the start of the 20th century drugs were still only inspected visually - no formal testing of content had been introduced. The druggist still made virtually everything in the shop with less than 10 per cent of all prescriptions being for 'proprietary' or brand name medicines - by 1933 this had

Top left: *Mill stones used for grinding poisonous roots.* *Top right:* *Workers gather outside the Company's Fleet Street premises, 1890s.* *Above:* *The Hanover Street Printing Counter, circa 1900.*

increased to 30 per cent. At this time Evans' was expanding into new areas: veterinary supplies, shop fittings and the supply of equipment for use in pharmacies, surgeries and operating theatres.

The start of the second world war in 1939 began auspiciously for the Evans' Company with orders from the government for anti tetanus serum and anti gangrene serum for the armed forces. During the Blitz the Hanover Street premises were destroyed, the damage was so severe that even store rooms 40 feet below street level were destroyed. Evans' staff were temporarily housed in the Liver Building.

After the sudden death of James Herbert E Evans, Ian V L Fergusson (great, great-grandson of the founder) is appointed Chairman after starting with the Company in 1919 as an apprentice.

As a result of the bombing, the Liverpool business moved from its premises in the city centre to a purpose built factory on a 30 acre site in Speke. This was also the start of manufacture of 'ethical pharmaceuticals' for the Company which was now able to proceed with no further major disasters and plan for the post war years. And what years they would prove to be.

In 1945 the name of the parent company changed to Evans Medical Supplies.

In 1946, at the close of the second world war the government announced plans for a National Health Service that will be free for all. This came about in 1948 along with free prescriptions and sickness and maternity benefits. In the first year 200 million NHS prescriptions were dispensed, almost double the number anticipated. Not even the cost saving measure of introducing prescription charges just a few years later of one shilling per prescription could stem the demand for medicines, a tide which Evans' took at the flood.

Unlike the decades which followed the first world war, the late 1940s and 50s were not years of economic depression even if they were years of austerity. Evans was able to employ more staff and increase production. In 1948 a Sterile Products plant was opened at Speke, in 1952 new offices on the first floor of the main building were occupied whilst in the following year a power station was built to provide steam for use in manufacturing. Mechanisation of the plant had been carefully planned and more than 1,000 orders were being handled each day with up to 14 vans being loaded simultaneously with some of the 20,000 items on the Company's product list. By now ten

Above: *Edward Evans Jnr (left) and John James Evans.*

Left and below left: *Examples of shopfittings supplied by Evans.*
Below: *James Herbert Evans.*

million bottles were being used each year.

Many former employees will have happy memories of this period and will recall for example the opening of a branch of the National Provincial Bank on the Speke site in 1956 and remember joining the various social clubs such as bowls, football, cycling, swimming, tennis, chess and photography.

Evans' were appointed the sole distributors in the UK of the polio vaccine in 1958 when this vaccine was distributed around the country in a large scale vaccination programme for the first time.

The Company celebrated its 150th anniversary in 1959, a year which was marked by the erection of new research labs (now Evans vaccines) on land to the east of the Speke works as well as making a name change to Evans Medical Ltd. By then more than 20 million containers were being used annually by the 1,178 staff working on the site and delivered in a fleet of 106 delivery vans.

But not everything was rosy. Since the early 1900s when drugs were first officially tested they were still only inspected visually - no formal testing of content had been introduced. By the 1960s lack of control in drug manufacture and their release by the international pharmaceutical industry had caused a number of deaths and other health problems. Now as a result of this, new rules and guidelines were developed and power was given to governing bodies in the UK and USA to monitor new drug developments and to assess facilities and procedures for producing and releasing new drugs into the marketplace. The Federal Drugs Administration in the USA and the Medicines Control Agency in the UK were now responsible for approving all new licences and monitoring clinical trials before the drug reached the consumer. These bodies also conducted

audits in pharmaceutical companies to ensure that all expected standards were met, if not exceeded.

In 1961, the year the Fleet Street premises were demolished, the Company was bought by Glaxo for £8.4 million but continued to trade as Evans Medical - albeit as a member of the Glaxo Group.

Both 1961 and 1962 were years of world-wide health scares but Evans' rose to the challenge. In 1961 a cholera epidemic swept Hong Kong but Evans' was able to supply 14,000 doses of vaccine within 24 hours. The following year, when smallpox appeared in England, the Company was able to provide a normal year's output in a single week helped by staff working round the clock.

The 1970s was a decade marked by industrial unrest

Above (both pictures): *Bomb damage during the war years.* *Far left: A 1960s Laboratory.* *Left: Princess Margaret visits the Speke site in 1966.*

across the whole of Britain. Evans' was not immune from the national trend and in 1974, 800 workers walked out on strike in support of a colleague who had allegedly been dismissed for the offence of being 'clocked on' by another worker. The strike lasted four days; fortunately such events would not become commonplace and by 1976 the Evans Aerosol Unit which had opened in July 1975 had packed its millionth aerosol spray on schedule.

It was in 1978 that Evans became part of Glaxo Operations. For the first time in more than 170 years the Company no longer bore the name of its founder - it was now simply known as Glaxo.

Ten years later Glaxo could claim to be the world's second largest pharmaceutical company with annual sales of £2,059 million and 35,000 employees across the globe. Such sales were not however helped that year when lightning struck at Speke putting the switchboard out of action and virtually isolating the site from the outside world: internal and external phones as well as computer terminals were all knocked out in a communications black out which lasted most of the day. Ironically the work on installing a new digital phone system to replace the site's 30 year old system had been completed only a few weeks previously.

Following the merger of Glaxo and Wellcome in 1995 the factory signs were changed once again - this time to Glaxo Wellcome.

The most recent change in the Company's identity came in January 2001 which saw the merger of Glaxo Wellcome and SmithKline Beecham. The new name would be GlaxoSmithKline creating a world leader in research and pharmaceutical manufacture and supply - and making Speke one of 108 factories in 41 countries world-wide. Sadly the creation of the new international conglomerate would result in proposals to close the Speke plant. Whatever the future might hold however, after so many years in Liverpool, those who have worked there over the decades will never forget the comradeship and goodwill which has so characterised this remarkable business and which has grown from such modest beginnings in the 19th century.

Top right: *The visit of Margaret Thatcher in 1976.* **Top left:** *An aerial view of the site in the 1980s.* **Above left:** *A Glaxo truck heading off on a delivery.* **Left:** *The new GlaxoSmithKline sign on the Company's Speke site.*

Blue Coat School
Changes and challenges
1708 - 2002

Our schooldays. Supposedly the best days of our lives, and certainly the longest since most of us could not wait for the bell to end each one of them! Some of us stayed on at our local school until the age of just 14 before leaving for the world of work. Other, somewhat younger, readers may have attended a 'Secondary Modern' or a brand new Comprehensive school. Still others may have passed their eleven plus and gone to a Grammar school. And some will have attended a school which can trace its history across three centuries - Liverpool's Blue Coat School.

In fact there are numerous Blue Coat Schools throughout the country. The earliest and most famous is Christ's Hospital in the City of London (now removed to Horsham Surrey) which was founded in 1563.

After the Reformation, when the monasteries were swept away, many public services such as health and education, which until then had been provided by the church, also disappeared.

Above: An 18th century sketch inside the old Blue Coat School. *Below:* A scene from outside Blue Coat Hospital on St George's Day 1843.

There was an urgent need for foundling hospitals and in answer to that need Christ's Hospital in London was founded - a place where poor children could be accommodated, cared for and taught. Blue is not a royal colour - that is purple, but it is the colour of alms-giving and charity. It was the common colour for clothes in Tudor times and so the charity children were dressed in blue Tudor frock coats, yellow stockings and white neck-bands at the throat. The children of the Liverpool Blue Coat School, both boys and girls would wear a distinctive, and archaic, uniform until 1948 when the 'Hospital' became a day and boarding school for boys.

The Liverpool Blue Coat Hospital was founded in 1708 by local merchant Bryan Blundell and the school's first headmaster, the Reverend Robert Stythe, to teach poor children how 'to read, write and cast accounts'.

Bryan Blundell was a master mariner and part or sole owner of the ship Mulberry then engaged in 'the foreign trade'. Robert Stythe was the first joint Rector of Liverpool.

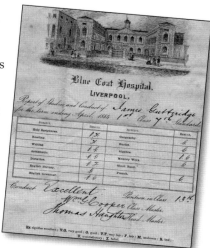

It was a time when there was no Welfare State but the great merchants in the area had a social conscience and the foundation rapidly grew as an orphanage for Liverpool boys and girls.

The original building was situated at Blue Coat Chambers in School Lane on land which had earlier been occupied by Cross' Free Grammar School. The land on which the school was built - then part of the waste near St Peter's churchyard - was granted by the Corporation and it was from this small school, built at the cost of just £35, that what was previously New Street took its new name - School Lane. Some 50 children were clothed and taught by the charity at this new day school, but fed and housed by their parents.

Bryan Blundell however took the view that out of school hours children were apt to get into bad habits and he therefore determined to change the school into one which took boarders; he immediately subscribed £750 with the promise of more to improve the school. In 1719 the foundation stones of fine new buildings were laid; built in the Queen Anne style the buildings still function today as the Bluecoat Arts Centre. Building continued until 1725 by which time the total cost had amounted to £2,288 - almost all raised by donations.

Pupil numbers remained at about 50, made up of both boys and girls, but by the closing years of the 18th century numbers had risen to 375 boarders, many of whom were required to contribute to the schools coffers and earn their keep by working at spinning or pin-making.

Top right: *A student report from 1884.* ***Above left:*** *Dining in the 1870s.* ***Left:*** *Cricket in the early 20th century.*

O Griffin a Liverpool sculptor and architectural carver.

The chapel was built from designs of the same architects who were responsible for the school building. The style is the late English Renaissance and is octagonal in form with a circular dome and transepts on three sides. The internal fittings are all oak, the walls being lined with bath stone. The Chapel can accommodate about 500 people and was dedicated by the Lord Bishop of Liverpool in 1906.

Life was undoubtedly quite tough for those early pupils, though some were prepared to rebel: on 25th July 1800 for example no fewer than 107 of the boys escaped for the day to visit Liverpool Fair after they had removed a door catch.

In 1899 two of the Trustees placed at the disposal of the Hospital a site of some seven and a half acres on the edge of Wavertree Playground. Some £80,000 was still needed for a new school building however, but one of the Trustees, WH Shirley, left the whole of his estate of £38,000 to the school and this, together with other gifts, enabled the work to proceed - as a result the school assembly hall is named the Shirley Hall in honour of the benefactor. The new building was designed by Messrs. Briggs, FB Hobbs and Arnold Thornley in the late renaissance style, and built by Morrison & Sons of Liverpool. Then, in 1908, in its bicentennial year, the whole school removed to new premises in what was then the quiet village of Wavertree. The area still retains a village atmosphere with its coaching inns, green and lock-up.

Another 'treasure' is the Board Room which belongs to the Foundation Trustees and is used for Governors' meetings and special occasions. In the Board Room one will find historic paintings, recently restored - some by an old boy, Richard Ansdell RA.

One of the greatest treasures of the school is its chapel. The beautiful Fenwick-Harrison Memorial Chapel was built in the early years of the 20th century by T Fenwick-Harrison as a memorial to his late wife. The chapel remains in daily use for morning assembly and is built in the baroque style with the faces of stone cherubs looking down - each one different and carved by Edward

Top left: The Brass Group circa 1910. *Above right:* East front before the Tower had been built, 1912. *Right:* Girls preparing for war duty.

Meanwhile Liverpool was being attacked by German bombers. The school at Wavertree was struck by incendiary bombs in May 1941, one of which set fire to the laundry and caused considerable damage. But though the buildings may have been saved when the school returned to Wavertree it came back to a very different post-war situation than the one it had left.

In 1949 Liverpool Education Authority approached the Governors of the Hospital with a proposals that the Hospital should become a two-form entry Voluntary Aided school for boys with boarding provision for those who needed it. Girls would no longer be part of the reformed school, and with them went the distinctive uniforms which had been such a memorable part of the school and in their place arrived the more conventional blue blazers.

The school has remained in Wavertree since 1908, except for the period of the second world war: then the school with its 270 boys and girls was evacuated to Beaumaris in Anglesey North Wales where it remained until 1947.

In June 1940 the school buildings in Wavertree were requisitioned by the War Office and arrangements were made for pupils, staff and furniture to be carried to Anglesey. By then, due to conscription, the male staff was reduced to the Headmaster, Senior Master and one assistant master: Mistresses were appointed to fill the vacancies.

Initially pupils were taught in the Church Hall at Beaumaris and were billeted on the local community but in 1941 the school rented Red Hill House from Sir Richard Bulkley where all the girls and a number of junior boys were installed. Later, other temporary accommodation would be found, such as a house known as 'Bryn' and a disused Wesleyan Chapel in Church Street. Finally a beautiful house 'Woodgarth' which lay alongside the Menai Straits was bought by the Trustees at a very reasonable price from the executors of FF Tattersall a generous friend of the school.

The Governors decided in 1959 to draw up a programme for additions and extensions to the school in order to bring it into line with modern educational requirements. That programme would be complete by 1964. As a result four new and very pleasant classrooms, four modern and exceptionally well equipped laboratories, a spacious well-stocked library, a music room with new furniture and a piano, a new asphalted yard, and, perhaps the most popular addition of all, a new swimming pool were added to the facilities and amenities of the school. Nor was the Boarding House forgotten and the Governors, at a cost of £14,000, constructed ten new studies in a separate building in the South Quadrangle; the luxurious studies were furnished as a result of the generous gift of £550 from the Old Blues; a tuck shop was also added to the amenities of the Boarding side.

Top: Formal Assembly in the Shirley Hall, 1930s.
Above: *Pupils modelling the old (pre 1948) School uniforms.*

In these years following the end of the second world war the Boarding House was full, mainly from service families, boys who needed boarding facilities due to home circumstances, local boys with parents working abroad and a group from the seamen's orphanage which had closed. It was real communal living, with open dormitories and bathroom. Bathing had to be strictly controlled as hot water was limited, being provided by an antiquated coal-fired boiler with Lewis, an 80 year old ex-naval stoker, permanently in the boiler house. Happy days - even if discipline was strict

Above: Old and new uniforms on display, 1949.
Right: Workshops in the 1950s.
Below: Inspecting the Cadet Force in the North Yard, 1950s. Below right: The unveiling of a plaque in memory of Dorothy Smith, a former senior mistress of the School from 1927 to 1947, by the Lady Mayoress and the Headmaster of the School, Mr GG Watcyn, 1951.

and everyone was up by 6.45 am and in bed by 9.30 pm; whilst being seen outside school without one's cap was a punishable offence.

By 1967 the total number of boys in the school was 518 but this included only a very small sixth form. Peter Arnold-Craft was appointed Headmaster in 1968 and he was instrumental in transforming the school into what it is today. His influence is still felt and pervades the work of the current Headmaster.

Another major change took place in 1989 when, forty years after they had been excluded, girls were re-admitted to the school to study in the sixth form. By 1995 the school would have 787 boys and 73 girls.

In July 1990 however, by which time the number of boarders had dropped to 29, boys boarding provision came to an end and the Governors proposed to the Department of Education that the school become a four-form entry.

September 1991 saw that proposal accepted and 30 more boys entered 'Year seven' or first form. To accommodate the increase in numbers a phased building expansion programme was put in place. The first phase saw the introduction of four new classrooms, two new laboratories and a new art room. Phase two, which began in 1993, saw the conversion of the former boarding wing into further classrooms and specialist teaching areas. Part of the improvements would be funded by the generous bequest of £159,000 from the estate of Mrs Doris Croston after whom the school library would be renamed.

Phase Three, which began in 1994, saw the creation of new laboratories and other improved facilities. In April 1998 the school received over seven million pounds from the New Deal for Schools initiative with a further £1.2 million from the School Foundation to refurbish the building.

In recent times, under the leadership of Sandy Tittershill a teacher at the school since 1966, the Blue Coat School has regularly featured amongst the top schools in the country. In August 2002 the school will embark on a massive multi-million pound building programme which will include ten new laboratories, a sports hall, music centre and a new dining hall. A new sixth form centre will also be created as well as a new library and resources area. Girls will be admitted into year 7 in September 2002 for the first time since 1949.

Though buildings, staff and pupils have changed endlessly over the course of three centuries one thing however remains constant: a commitment to academic excellence underpinned by that school motto - Non sibi sed omnibus - not for oneself but for all.

Top: *The School Chapel.*
Left: *The School Clock Tower today.*
Below: *Mr Sandy Tittershill, Headmaster.*
Below right: *The Blue Coat School Crest.*

Taxi!

'Taxi!' Somehow the very word is exciting, conjuring up as it does visions of important journeys or special occasions. A taxi ride is so often the start of a journey to the docks, railway station or airport; no wonder we love them. And flagging down a black cab with rain threatening and experiencing the relief of knowing one will arrive at ones destination without getting soaked is a happy recollection for all of us.

Even the Americans have recognised the unique place taxis have in our collective unconscious and gave us a television series simply entitled! Taxi!

Though most of us associate taxis with the era of the motor car they are really much older than that: licensed hackney cabs, the horse drawn equivalent of the taxi, were familiar enough in Victorian England; and the standard design of the modern black cab still reflects this with its internal height being sufficient for a gentleman to sit without having to remove his top hat - and a turning circle every bit as good as a two-wheeled carriage. The name 'taxi' comes to us as a shortened version of the French word 'taximetre' or tariff meter, the first modern use of a fixed rate per mile for travel having become popular in Paris before finding its way over the Channel to us. The taximeter was a welcome innovation saving the travelling public from the nuisance of having to negotiate every fare, and saved many a cab driver from having to argue about the size of the fare - well, it saved him some arguing, though most taxi drivers have tales to tell of customers who still disputed the fare that was staring them in the face from the implacable meter.

In fact the taximeter is far older even than the version used by Parisian carriage drivers having been invented in Greco-Roman times using a cogged wheel linked to the axle of carriages for hire in the north African city of Alexandria well before the birth of Christ.

Below: *A group of taxi drivers on a day out to Blackpool, circa 1945-46.*

MERSEYSIDE RADIO   METER CABS LTD.

Registered Office :
164a HEYWORTH STREET, LIVERPOOL 5
Telephone ANField 3465

The idea of the taximeter disappeared in the centuries following the collapse of the Roman Empire and the ending of civilisation as they new it. Fortunately for the world, and the inhabitants of Liverpool in particular, both civilisation and the taximeter would eventually return.

More than any other provincial city Liverpool and Liverpudlians love their taxis. Strangers to the City will often express surprise that we appear to have so many taxis on our roads compared to other cities. Why that should be is something of a mystery. Perhaps it is a legacy of the city's unusual history as a major port and the need for fleets of cabs to move passengers from railway terminals to the docks and back again. Or perhaps it was the episodic affluence of returning seamen with ready cash who fuelled demand. Who knows why, but what we can be certain of is that our love affair with taxis shows no sign of ending, even if the flood of passengers and seamen to and from the docks has long since ended.

Today the most familiar name in the taxi business in Liverpool is Mersey Cabs. Back in 1998 Mersey Cabs, probably one of the largest cab companies in Britain outside London, celebrated its 40th birthday. The company which today provides 24 hour a day service to its customers in the Liverpool and Merseyside areas prides itself on its 'Be Safe, Be Secure with Mersey Cabs' motto.

Top: Annual summer outing to Blackpool, circa 1950.
Above: A 1950s company letter head.

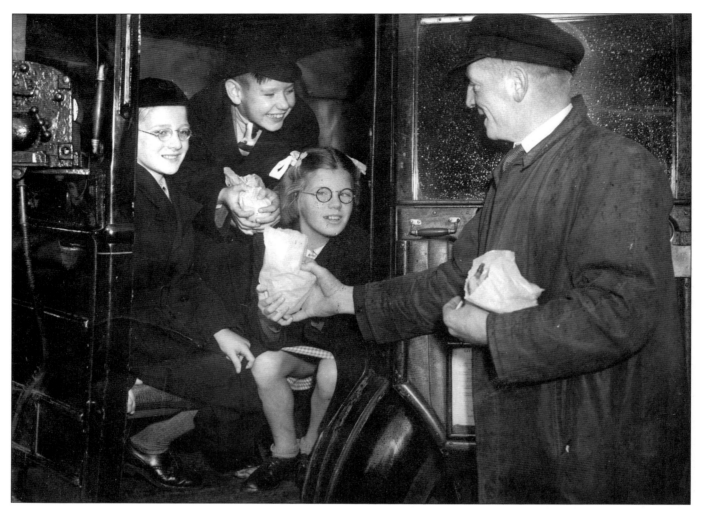

All drivers are licensed and vetted by Liverpool City Council ensuring the safety of all passengers; that stringent vetting of all drivers also includes police checks and women travelling alone have no need to fear about their safety with Mersey Cabs.

Today details of all calls, including time, location, of pick-ups, destination and driver allocated are stored on computer. Wheelchair access is provided in all vehicles, which have wide-opening doors to allow easy access for mothers with prams and pushchairs whilst many vehicles also have swivel seats for ease of getting in and out along with an additional step and even wheelchair ramps for wheelchair users.

Mersey Cabs prides itself on offering a fast efficient service and aims to respond to all calls within ten minutes. With 13 incoming telephone lines and three telephonists on duty at any one time this seems quite likely.

Those telephonists are backed up by two 'despatchers' whose intimate knowledge of the city is legendary, whilst the radio room itself is staffed by 27 people.

Today the fleet of more than 400 taxis represents around a third of all licensed taxis in Liverpool and services cover not only Merseyside but nation-wide.

It was in the late 1950s mobile radio communications units were first installed into a few Liverpool hackney carriage vehicles, including some in Bootle, Crosby and Litherland cabs, by a well known company of that day. This meant that for the first time the public at large were able to telephone a cab rather than go on the streets to hail one.

And what cabs they were in those days. Are you old enough to remember the taxis of that era? Can you recall those post-war days of pre-war cabs, of leather seats and a space beside the driver large enough to take a full cabin trunk of luggage rather than the far smaller suitcases we now seem to all content ourselves with now that we'll be charged extra on the plane to Majorca?

Top: *The first outing of the Blind Childrens Committee to Southport in 1950. Prior to leaving driver Jimmy Connor distributes sweets and fruit to the children.*

What a joy to get into a taxi back then and innocently light up an untipped cigarette and enjoy the unfettered luxury of no seat belt; didn't we feel like toffs as we cruised down the road only cursing momentarily as the rattling over the cobblestones knocked the cigarette ash on to our trousers and on to the floor. Not that the cabby minded ash on the floor, in those days more often than not the driver too would be contentedly puffing away on his Park Drive or Woodbine.

With the majority of work being done within the Liverpool City boundaries the use of radios brought home to the Liverpool taxi trade the necessity of forming a fleet of Liverpool cabs under a common title, all to be fitted with mobile radio units to cater for the growing number of telephone users. And so 'Mersey Cabs' was born. The first meeting of these new radio enthusiasts was held on 7th January 1958 when the acquisition of premises and the installation of radio equipment by Pye's Ltd was the main theme of the meeting.

The company 'Merseyside Radio Meter Cabs Limited' officially came into being on 20th January 1958; the directors at that time being Frank Foster (Chairman), Graham Read Snr (Treasurer), Jack Latham

(Secretary) along with Ray Baxter, Sid Bradley, Alf Daly, Norman Derrick, John Forsyth, Billy Mills, Bill Smith and Peter Timewell. All the directors and officers were confirmed in their appointments at a meeting held at the Victoria Hotel in Lime Street on Tuesday 4th March 1958.

In April 1958 agreement was reached to acquire premises at 164-166 Heyworth Street and the directors met there for the first time on 29th April.

By the following January the new company had installed radio units into over 50 cabs with a waiting list of other taxis ready to join the company as and when more radio units became available. It might be noted that even in those early days difficulty was being experienced in employing top class radio operators; it was soon proposed that the wages of the radio operators be increased to £10 per 48 hour week, a fair wage for those times and worth comparing with the £2.50 per week rent for radio rental.

At a board meeting held in September 1959 the directors were able to express not only their satisfaction at progress so far but some well founded optimism for the future.

Stan Gough became chairman in 1961. His tenure would be a long one. Having been shareholder from the outset Stan would remain chairman until 1986 when he would be elevated to company President.

Throughout the 1960s however, and half way through the 1970s, the company prospered to such an extent that it outgrew the

Top right and above left: *Letterheads from the 1970s.*
Left: *The Falkland Street Office.*

space available at Heyworth Street. An agreement by the directors to look for bigger premises resulted in the purchase of 171 Lodge Lane in Liverpool 8 where the company moved in the Autumn of 1975.

During the remainder of the 1970s and into the 1980s expansion continued with a second radio channel being introduced in 1985. This enabled the Merseyside area to be split between channel one and channel two. The number of cabs taking advantage of the radio units over that period increased from 200 to 300 and by 1990 would reach 480.

During the late half of the 1980s computer equipment was now installed in the general office, extra telephone lines were added and a third radio channel opened.

With such continued growth the President Stan Gough, and Directors, Tony Kidd, Graham Read, Doug Watts, Dave Griffith, Cliff McGoldrick, George Ross and Robert Stevenson decided that larger premises were again needed.

With a variety of proposals being made by bodies such as the City Council, the Department of Trade and various develop-ment agencies the decision was finally made to buy Abbey House, Falkland Street, Liverpool 3. After extensive decorating and re-fitting the company moved into its new offices on 21st May 1990.

With a hundred foot radio mast on site the transmission range would now reach well beyond the Merseyside area giving ample reception to all mobile units once the teething problems were sorted out.

Soon computerisation of the radio operation was complete too. This meant that all telephonists could now take details over the telephone and type them directly on to their computer screens which would then appear automatically on the screen of the area channel operator.

Further expansion into those areas not yet covered by Mersey Cabs was now envisaged to make full use of the new multi-channel radio units being fitted into all cabs.

From those early days when the first call was received by telephone and sent out over the airwaves to the nearest cab Mersey Cabs has grown to be one of Britain's largest radio cab companies outside of London. By 1990 Mersey Cabs would be despatching over 20,000 calls each week over its three radio channels.

And not just people were being ferried about the City. Almost from the outset Mersey Cabs has been offering business users a Special Express Delivery and Collection Service 24 hours a day, with quoted prices for deliveries given on request. Radio contact enables routes and pick-

Top right: *The Lodge Lane Office.* ***Above:*** *A variety of fare meters used by the firm over the years.*

ups to be altered, and the monitoring of goods in transit. Each client's deliveries being transported on an individual basis.

Since each driver has a comprehensive knowledge of the City this, combined with the driver's vouched for integrity, would ensure a safe and sure delivery of valuable and costly goods.

Furthermore each taxi is fitted with a sealed meter and is subject to regular checks by the City Council enforcement officers which removed the guess work on fares.

Clients can book in advance, make regular bookings or get a taxi immediately - for account holders the computer handles the information and produces monthly invoices on journeys done, whilst cash customers pay the driver in the normal away.

For large volume business users monthly invoices can be tailored to individual requirements with detailed invoices which give control of personal activity and expenditure. An account with Mersey Cabs means less paperwork,

fewer petty cash slips to process and less paper to clog up the system. Authorisation for taxi use can be controlled by a security number or password and invoices are sent out monthly.

Account customers get special treatment, and even have a hot line telephone number for their use when requesting a taxi. Account clients include hospitals, doctors, public authorities, banks, industrial and accountancy firms, hotels, small shops and large stores.

For almost half a century Merseyside Radio Meter Cabs has been providing a taxi service to the people of Liverpool. It's not an easy job and there are no days off with taxis available 24 hours a day 365 days a year. So let's show our appreciation the next time we call a taxi: when we finish our journey let's give a tip that reflects prices in the 21st century and not those of the 1950s when the business began!

MERSEY CABS LTD.

25th Anniversary

Dinner Dance

to be held at

DOVEDALE TOWERS
PENNY LANE

on

WEDNESDAY, 15th DECEMBER 1982

7.00 pm. ~ 1.00 am
EXTENSION LICENCE APPLIED FOR

TICKETS £12.00 each
AVAILABLE ONLY FROM MERSEY CABS OFFICE 171 LODGE LANE, L'POOL 8
(IT IS POSSIBLE TO PAY FOR THESE TICKETS WEEKLY, MONTHLY OR ALL AT ONCE)

DRESS: LOUNGE SUIT - COLLAR & TIE MUST BE WORN
EVENING DRESS OPTIONAL

Above: A poster advertising the firm's 25th Anniversary Dinner Dance in 1982.
Below: One of the company cabs pictured in 2002.

On the move

Sooner or later everyone has to move house. Just within living memory the very oldest amongst us may recall moving house and piling furniture in to the back of a horse-drawn cart or van. For most of us however moving has meant calling a modern removal firm to collect our tables and chairs, TVs and fridges and take them away in a high sided motor van especially designed for the job.

Around Liverpool one of the most familiar sights are the yellow liveried vans of the removal firm of John Mason International Ltd. And if you aren't old enough to recall removals being made by horse-drawn vehicles there were certainly many members of the Mason family whose memories went so far back.

The company was founded in 1884 by Mrs Mary Mason in Wavertree, a township then on the outskirts of Liverpool. Before starting out on her own Mary Mason had earlier helped her husband John in his carting business. When Mary's son, also John, began helping her in 1887 coal deliveries became the main activity. In 1890 Mary's, by then, 17 year old son took over and expanded the business into a general carrying. In that

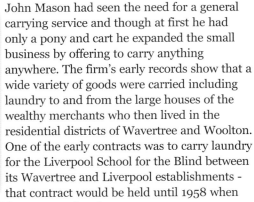

same year a contract was signed with a local company that was to last for 68 years.

John Mason had seen the need for a general carrying service and though at first he had only a pony and cart he expanded the small business by offering to carry anything anywhere. The firm's early records show that a wide variety of goods were carried including laundry to and from the large houses of the wealthy merchants who then lived in the residential districts of Wavertree and Woolton. One of the early contracts was to carry laundry for the Liverpool School for the Blind between its Wavertree and Liverpool establishments - that contract would be held until 1958 when the city establishment was closed.

John Mason married Mary Hannah Baker in 1897 and from then on she assisted her husband with the clerical and book

Above: Mrs Mary Mason outside her home in 85 High Street, Wavertree, 1900. The office was run from this house.
Below: John Mason with one of his first horse and carts.

The city of Liverpool was growing and as new districts were being developed contracts were obtained from the City Corporation to carry material to and from the new roads being constructed around the rapidly expanding city. John Mason was a man of great energy and enterprise never afraid of hard work - if necessary doing so round the clock. He also had a great passion for horses and his only hobby was buying and selling them for himself and for others. John Masons judgement was so respected that he bought and sold horses for a number of the principal dock contractors, and Lord Sefton even entrusted him with commissions to buy horses on his behalf. John would regularly spend a day each month at the Craven Arms Horse Repository and he was also keen on entering his horses in agricultural shows where his horses won many prizes.

By the outbreak of the first world war in 1914 John Mason had built up a thriving firm engaged in coal retailing, general haulage and household removals and, although the shortage of horses during the war, would restrict business John's astuteness ensured that the business did not falter.

In 1917 the business moved to 127, High Street, Wavertree gaining more space for both warehousing and stabling for the firm's horses.

keeping work she would later continue to do for her sons in their turn.

Soon more vehicles and heavier horses were acquired. Furniture vans were built to John Mason's requirements.

From the small firm's base at 85 High Street, the Mason family home, the first long distance removals were undertaken in 1900 using horse-drawn vehicles. Early customers included the Anglo American Oil Company which would become Esso, the Cheshire Lines Railway Company and the English Margarine Works.

When work started on the Liverpool Anglican Cathedral in 1904 the aptly named John Mason carried much of the carved stonework for Morrisons Ltd, the firm given the contract to build the Cathedral. Soon the firm's activities had extended not only to Liverpool but to Manchester, many parts of Lancashire, Cheshire and North Wales using horse-drawn vehicles, whilst longer distances, those over 50 miles, were covered by rail.

Top left: John Mason driving one of his first horse-drawn vans. A similar vehicle has been lent to Liverpool Transport Museum. Above left: 127 High Street - the second family home and office since the early 1920s. Right: One of the first motor vehicles to be purchased - French manufactured Aries.

John and Mary Mason's eldest son, Leslie, born in 1904 entered the business in his early teens, he would play a full part in the firm for almost fifty years. Leslie had shown an early interest in the business from childhood and at the age of only 12 was already helping by driving a pony and wagon like his father before him; by the age of 16 Leslie was driving a team of horses helping to overcome the wartime manpower shortage and enabling him to learn the business from a practical point of view.

In 1921, when the first motor vehicle was acquired, an Albion, it had solid tyres and a chain drive. Although more motor vehicles would be steadily added to the fleet horse transport would still be the main form of transport for some time, and more horses continued to be bought for many years. It would not be until almost the outbreak of the second world war that all horse-drawn vehicles would be replaced by motor vans, platform vehicles and lift vans. Meanwhile with the increasing help of Leslie Mason the business developed and its reputation for good workmanship and the personal attention and courtesy of its employees became ever more widely known.

By 1926 the first lift vans for rail were bought and overseas agents were appointed to look after the firm's interests abroad.

A year before the outbreak of the second world war in 1938 John Mason's second son Stanley joined the business. Born in 1921 Stanley would play a major role in developing the company but his practical training involving driving and packing was interrupted in 1941 by him being called up to serve in the Merchant Navy for the duration of the war.

Top: *One of the first Albion's, purchased c1921.*
Above: *Mason's first pneumatic tyred vehicle. A forerunner of the modern fleet.*

As in the first world war domestic moves were much reduced, though contracts gained from the government helped keep the business going despite both a manpower shortage and petrol rationing. The second world war which brought to an end the era of the horse-drawn vehicle saw the firm's motorised vehicles being called up for war service. One of the many interesting jobs undertaken was the continuous removal of the Royal Liverpool Philharmonic Orchestra's instruments around the country enabling it to continue to give regular performances. The orchestra gave many concerts to troops and civilians during the war years; Mason's driver Bill Clarke was never late for a concert even though he had to contend with all the hazards of the black out and enemy bombing.

During the war 'Masons' did vital work evacuating schools, institutions, government departments, commercial and industrial concerns and homes. Munitions and other war equipment were carried, whilst to meet the call for decentralisation extra warehouses were acquired on the outskirts of the city and at Penmaenmawr, in North Wales, for furniture storage.

Each evening Mason vehicles reported for duty at Civil Defence and Fire Posts. During the intense bombing of Liverpool the Mason team played its part.

The end of the war brought with it the enormous problems of rebuilding after the destruction of the blitz. Industry and commerce had to be reorganised to meet the needs of the post-war world. The Mason brothers, with hard work and foresight, made great progress. Large office removals were undertaken and a considerable contribution made to the transport services required by the vast rebuilding programme which would take place. Weeks of pre-planning were necessary in some cases for the removals of private and government offices to ensure the minimum disruption

Above: A vehicle permanently engaged in moving the musical instruments of the Philharmonic Orchestra around the country during the second world war.
Below: The drive-on drive-off service from Preston to Larne, Mason's were one of the first companies to use this service.

of office routine, and several had to be undertaken at weekends. Many hundreds of tons of files, papers and office equipment were involved in one of the largest moves during which the Inland Revenue, Ministry of Food and other Ministerial offices were moved from Llandudno to London.

In 1948 a daily removal service from Liverpool to London was started; London depot facilities would be eventually acquired from FL Pettman Ltd to facilitate distribution in the London area and return loading and by 1950 the company became one of the founder members of FIDI - the World-wide Federation of International Furniture Removers.

John Mason, who had retired at the end of the war, died in 1953 after which Leslie and Stanley became managing directors jointly running what was now a company. In 1948 the business had grown to such an extent that the private limited company of John Mason (Wavertree) Ltd had been formed with John and Mary Mason and their sons Leslie and Stanley as its directors. To ensure reliability all vehicles had always to be kept in first class condition so that delivery promises could be honoured. Now the fleet and equipment would be kept constantly up to date by the purchase of new vehicles. Steady expansion of Mason's service was made to cover the whole of the United Kingdom.

During 1955 a daily removal service to Ireland using the Preston/Larne Roll on-Roll off ferry commenced and, combined with the daily Liverpool/London service, offered the quickest route available from the capital to Ireland. Mason's would be one of the first removal firms to use the ferry service from Preston, and at the time the

only firm in the north west offering an almost daily service to Ireland of articulated trailer vans, a service offering considerable savings in packing and handling costs since loading on and off the ferry by cranes was no longer needed.

To give a more local service in Cheshire in 1955 Leslie and Stanley became directors of B Dudley & Sons Ltd - Removers of Bebington, a firm established in 1869 and both companies worked in close association. In 1959 Dudley's would be taken over completely by Masons.

By the closing years of the 1950s Masons, in association with four reputable South of England firms, had also

*Top: The fleet pictured in front of Liverpool Cathedral during the 1960s. **Inset:** Delivering a grand piano to the QEII. **Above right:** A horse drawn van being exhibited at Liverpool Show during the 1950s.*

established a network of distribution routes serving the Midlands, the South West, the South East and the South of England as well as many parts of Wales, Lancashire and Yorkshire.

In 1959 a new 16,000 sq. ft warehouse was opened in Wavertree, built to the company's specifications and specially designed and constructed to store customers' effects with the highest possible degree of safety. By 1962 the continued growth of the company resulted in the purchase of a 36,000 sq. ft warehouse in Kirby. The company launched into the antique shipping business which required large consolidation and storage facilities. By 1967 a further 2,000 sq. ft warehouse was acquired bringing the company's total Merseyside facilities to 72,000 sq.ft.

Stanley Mason was elected President of the Overseas Division of the British Association of Removers in 1965.

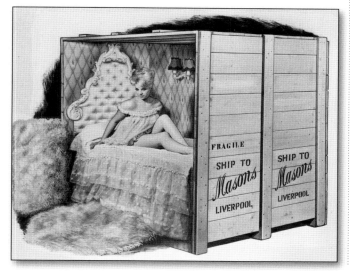

Sadly 1971 began with Leslie Mason's death, following which Stanley's wife, Jean, joined her husband as a director; they were joined in 1972 by their eldest son Paul.

In 1974 the company joined Eurovan, a consortium of around 180 mainly privately owned world wide removal companies and by 1977 a record volume of antique shipping was recorded - some 250 ISO containers were packed and despatched from the company's warehouses. By 1982 that success was consolidated with a record year for inter-continental removals: over 400 containers were exported winning the company the Eurovan 'Biggest Booker' award.

The following year, in April 1983, Stanley Mason died and his son Paul now joined his mother Jean as a director of the company.

More than a century of successful trading has been achieved not only through the hard work of the directors but very much because the company has always enjoyed a completely loyal and hard working staff. Their contribution above all else has played the central role in the growth and development of the business. It was in that spirit that the firm entered its second century in 1984.

In 1989 all the company's local activities were transferred to 35 Wilson Road, Huyton whilst a new warehouse and offices were opened in Croydon.

Today international, commercial and household moves and storage are at the core of the firm's business.

With the fourth generation of the Mason family, Paul Mason, now at the helm of this prestigious removal firm Mason's currently facilitates over 8,000 removals each year across the globe.

From a single horse and cart and undertaking only local work, during the course of many decades the firm of John Mason International Ltd has grown into a major player on the world stage. But despite its massive growth the firm has still managed to retain the virtues of a small family firm: flexibility, a genuine appreciation of its employees and an unswerving commitment to meeting its clients' needs.

Above left: *Mason's won first prize in an FIDI photography competition in the section entitled "A Most Beautiful Removal".*
Left: *A Mason's van and trailer pictured in front of the Liver Building, 1958.*

All that gas

Today the gas industry is recognised as being modern and go-ahead but in the 1950s it was in the doldrums, suffering from its Victorian image of gas lights and old fashioned stoves. In those days before North Sea Gas the industry was almost totally dependant upon coal for the manufacture of 'town' gas and successive increases in the price of suitable coal would have led to gas pricing itself out of the market.

The gas industry was looking for ways to revitalise itself: not only was the search for natural gas going ahead off the coast of Britain but by the mid 1960s plans would reach fruition to import liquid gas from North African countries in huge ocean going tankers.

At the same time as new methods of gas production were being looked at, gas appliance manufacturers were taking a hard look at their products and bringing them into line with contemporary needs. One such far sighted firm was Liverpool's Robinson Willey.

Great strides were being made in design, especially in room heaters which not only had to provide warmth and comfort but also be desirable objects of furniture in their own right.

The gas industry's revival in the North West was soon obvious: the value of gas appliance sales in 1958 had totalled £4.2 million whilst by 1965 sales had increased to £11.4 million after being given a considerable boost by the renewed interest in clean air.

The story of Robinson Willey began in the 1860s when two separate companies were founded: Robinsons of Liverpool and Willey's of Exeter.

Founded by Joseph H Robinson in 1869, Robinsons was originally engaged in stove enamelling work, but as the business developed a brass foundry was added which produced various components for the gas industry, including enamelled gauges for gas meters.

The firm started life in very humble premises in Grafton Street. As the business developed it moved to larger premises in North Hill Street in the 1880s.

Following the outbreak of the first world war in 1914 the firm, now JH Robinson and Co Ltd, switched production to munitions and larger premises were

Below: *The J H Robinson & Co (Liverpool) Ltd in Mill Lane as it was in the 1950s.*

acquired at Mill Lane, Old Swan in Liverpool - the company's main site to the present day.

Chairman of Robinsons in the years immediately following the end of the first world war was George Henry Robinson; before the war he had spent several years sheep farming in Australia whilst his elder brother ran Robinsons. After having served in the war and having risen from trooper to the rank of captain he returned to England on his brother's death to run the family firm.

The years following the Great War were ones of expansion and development with the addition of a hot brass stamping shop in 1925. Despite the economic recession of the 1930s, which hit most firms badly, even more expansion became necessary at Robinsons and in 1933 the company was able to acquire the adjacent premises and gain some much needed space. At this time the firm was making all types of meters and later gas geysers, test holders, 'governors', 'indices', brass unions and hot pressings.

Despite growth the firm was however still one in which managers were as skilled as the men they employed. According to one story the Chairman, by then Mr Sandford Robinson, and the works manager, William Jones, learnt late one Friday that some samples of a new hot forging were required by a customer for the following Monday. The tool room staff said the sample could not possibly be produced in time. Nothing daunted the chairman and works manager set to work on their own. Over the weekend without any assistance they went through the complete process of cutting steel blocks, turning the necessary dies, sinking and hardening, setting in to the hot stamping press, cutting the 'billets' and finally finishing the samples which the customer did indeed receive on the following Monday morning. Those were the days!

By 1937, when war clouds were gathering over Europe, Robinsons was already devoting some of its production capacity to munitions work. When war finally broke out in 1939 the firm switched almost all its capacity to the war effort as the plant was ideally suited to the manufacture of sheet metal pressings, fuse stamping and complete fuses.

During the war Robinsons' work ranged from making parts weighing just a few ounces to several pounds. Whilst the majority of components were destined for communications equipment of some kind other work was for use in tanks or aircraft. Many hundreds of thousands of stampings were supplied to Royal Ordnance factories throughout Great Britain.

Robinsons was also one of the few concerns able to produce complete fuses right from the manufacture of the brass rod itself.

*Above: The opening of a new factory and office block by W Hodkinson Esq O.B.E, in June 1960. **Left:** Some of the 10cwt Morgan lip-pouring hydraulic oil-fired furnaces in operation in the foundry, 1965.*

The varied output went into rifle bullets, tracers and explosive shells for Army field guns and Naval guns, anti-aircraft guns and rockets. Other war work of note included making camera spools for reconnaissance planes and even special lighters for the use of men abroad.

The other half of today's famous name, Willey's, would also have a distinguished war record.

Willey's was established in Exeter in 1861 by HF Willey. Originally involved in the woollen industry Willey later entered the engineering business to begin the production of gas manufacturing plant and ancillary equipment, light foundry work and other component engineering for the gas industry. Willey's became a public limited company in 1865. The firm's founder became a prominent citizen being an Alderman of Exeter; he was later a Sheriff of the city and was elected Mayor in 1893 shortly before his death in the following year when the founder's son, Henry Willey, took over as chairman and led the business into an era of expansion.

Willey's 'claim to fame' would be the launch of the first 'coin in the slot' gas meter developed by one of the firm's directors, Steffen Simpson in the early 1900s. From the 1900s onwards Willey's and the gas industry came to be closely associated. The company manufactured gas plant in its entirety, even covering the complete installation of gas works.

By 1930 Willey's was engaged in iron and steel construction work of many types including huge gas holders, iron roofs, bridges and the manufacture of gas and other 'illuminants' and employed almost 1,000 men. Following several years of expansion the employment figures had risen to 1,380 people and each year 125,000 gas meters were being made or repaired at the firm's Exeter works.

Top: A general view of the production shop at the Robinson Willey works in the 1960s. **Above right:** A typical showroom in the 1960s.

But now however the threat of war loomed once again in Europe and in July 1939 Willey's started to manufacture depth charge firing pistols for the Admiralty. When war did come Willey's played its part to the full producing a tremendous range of war material.

In producing munitions Willey's was extremely active in both world wars. One of the firm's proudest achievements was to be associated with the manufacture of the 'Mulberry Harbours' the artificial floating harbours which when towed across the English Channel would play such an important role in the Allied armies D-Day landings in Normandy in the Summer of 1944.

Robinsons and Willey's were destined to eventually become associated when in 1929 their parent company, United Gas

Industries Ltd, came into being, a group which also included Smiths Meters of Streatham in London. The two firms merged to form Robinson Willey Ltd however only in 1962.

The merger was the catalyst for a dramatic expansion in the field of gas water heaters and gas fires. It was decided to create separate companies again in 1966 in order to specialise in different fields with the group, meter business returning to Streatham leaving Liverpool's Robinson Willey to become a market leader in the field of domestic heating appliances and to fully justify its unique slogan: Robinson Willey - the hottest name in gas!

By now the company chairman was Sir Leonard Owen CBE; he had been associated not in fact with gas but with atomic energy since 1946, and had played a major part in the implementation of the nuclear power programme in Britain. Sir Leonard however resigned from his executive responsibilities with the Atomic Energy Authority in 1962 to go into industry.

Growth was the order of the day; with a massive switch to gas heating already underway a new factory was built at a cost of £175,000 on a piece of land previously occupied by a temporary structure containing the firm's laboratory. The 50,000 square feet of floor space would provide ample room for expansion. That project would mean a considerable increase in the work force. Work on the new building had begun in January 1965 with the two-storey building completed by the end of the year.

Top left: The company installed two 400 tonne capacity power presses for the manufacture of larger and high volume components in the early 1990s. *Left:* The recently introduced flow-line manufacturing plant dedicated to the company's flagship product range - The Firegem Visa. *Below:* One of the two powder coat plants which have been installed at the Old Swan manufacturing site, which use sophisticated paint technology to paint decorative gas fire components.

The main section of the Robinson Willey works however was still devoted to the production of plumbers' brasswork and to engineering brasswork of all types. More than 3,000 different brass items were being produced for use on land, sea and air as well as underground with many products used in making mining equipment.

The large range of plumbing fittings included waste outlets for baths, wash basins and sinks whilst the company was also supplying components to the makers of fire extinguishers, immersion heaters, washing machines, fridges and motor vehicles as well as to the gas industry.

Since the 1960s, Robinson Willey's name has been synonymous with high-efficiency radiant/ convector gas fires owing to the worldwide popularity of its Firegem Visa 2 range. Whilst the company still retains an enviable lead in this market sector over the years it has continuously developed a range of gas fires designed to meet evolving installation requirements, safety designs and tastes in consumer fashion.

Hence, the company today boasts a growing portfolio of fires suitable for both mains and LP gas including outset and inset living flame fires together with balanced flue gas models suitable for homes without a chimney. The company also offers a range of balanced flue gas wall heaters suitable for both domestic and commercial installation.

Continuously looking to expand its product base and venture into new markets, the company launched its first

Top left: Managing Director, Colin Pemberton at the launch of the firm's new Corporate Identity in 1995. Above right: Robinson Willey exhibiting in the USA in 2001. Right: Robinson Willey's best-selling radiant/convector gas fire the Firegem Visa 2 range.

electric fire in 1998 and since then has gone on to develop a wide range of models, many with gas equivalents.

Through Robinson Willey's sister-company, GrateGlow Fires, the company also offers a popular range of high-efficiency gas and electric fires, including a best-selling range of basket style gas fires. Acquired in the early 1990s by Robinson Willey's parent Group, Carver plc, the GrateGlow brand has enabled Robinson Willey to widen its product range and distribution base within the retail sector for fires and fireplaces.

The firm has always been renowned for its pioneering developments in the field of gas fire safety and indeed, was the first manufacturer to introduce a 'Safeguard' safety system to its entire gas fire range (excluding balanced flue models) that offers consumers valuable protection against blocked flues and inadequate ventilation. Since then, RW has gone on to introduce 'Safeguard Calibrator' - a unique safety tester for the Safeguard system and a revolutionary integral Carbon Monoxide detector for its best-selling Firegem Visa 2 range of gas fires.

Following the demise of British Gas on the high street in 1999, RW realised the need to adapt and acclimatise to changing market conditions and diversify its product portfolio. In addition to restructuring its distribution base via merchants and independent distributors, the company looked to diversify into new markets. It was during this same year that the company also acquired Linquartz Ltd - a leading manufacturer of quartz linear heaters - and so began the foray into new commercial and industrial heating sectors.

Since 1999, the company has extended its range of commercial and industrial heating appliances to include a portfolio of electric and dynamic storage heaters, electric panel heaters, air curtains and a range of air cleaning systems. In order to strengthen its growing presence within the electrical wholesale sector, the company has also recently introduced a comprehensive range of direct heating appliances that incorporates oil-filled radiators, fan and convector heaters, towel rails and down flow

heaters suitable for bathrooms and kitchens.

The foray into new market sectors is not, however, at the expense of Robinson Willey's established markets. Indeed, the company continues to flourish in the sector for gas and electric fires and is set to launch a new range of gas fires with remote controls, a multi-flue gas fire and for the first time ever, a complimentary range of fire surrounds.

Such market expansion and product development has only been made possible by Robinson Willey's continuous investment in state-of-the-art manufacturing, research and development facilities at its manufacturing site in Old Swan, the same site where it all began over 40 years ago. Indeed, over recent years, the company has invested several million in advanced research and manufacturing facilities.

Robinson Willey also continues to take on new global challenges and over the years has widened its export base to include North America, Europe and Australia. The recent appointment of the company's first-ever Export Manager looks set to ensure that Robinson Willey will go on to increase its presence on the worldwide stage.

From its origins in the 1860s Liverpool's Robinson Willey can look back on a century and a half with pride. The two firms which came together in the 1960s, a century after they began their corporate existence, have made an extraordinary contribution to many lives. By adapting to market changes, Robinson Willey has not only survived where so many others have failed, but it has indeed prospered. With a turnover in excess of £14 million and employing a local work force of over 200, Robinson Willey has become a flagship for Liverpool enterprise. With an overriding passion to succeed, the future looks more than bright.

Top left: *Following the firm's recent diversification into new electrical markets the sales team has been strengthened by John Young, Mark Adams, Paul Glover and Simon Chapman.* ***Left:*** *In early 2002 the firm was appointed by Mr Electric - to supply a comprehensive range of electric heating appliances to the company's network of franchise locations throughout the UK. Robinson Willey's Marketing Executive, Tracey Falshaw is pictured with Clive Houlston, Mr Electric's UK Franchise Director and Robinson Willey's Sales Manager, John Francis, at the rear.*

Doorknobs and broomsticks

The world of shopping has undergone remarkable changes over the last forty years or so. In 1960 supermarkets and out of town stores were unknown. For most of us shopping meant trailing from shop to shop, each more often than not owned by a sole trader, many of whom would still pick items off the shelf behind them and put them on the counter as we asked for them: self service was still a concept we had yet to come to terms with.

When it came to ironmongery, DIY and gardening goods the story was very much the same. If we wanted nails we went to the local ironmonger who would weigh out our nails by the pound from a large tub and hand them to us in a brown paper bag. And as for garden centres, well there were none, we bought seeds at Woolies and forks and trowels from the market. The idea of huge, open-plan stores with massive car parks was inconceivable. It was hardly surprising that such things were inconceivable - after all how many of us owned cars back then?

DIY has become immensely popular having been promoted endlessly on television, from Barry Bucknall in the 1960s to more recent programmes like changing Rooms and Groundforce. The demand seems almost unlimited and at every weekend thousands of us are beavering away beautifying our homes and gardens. Popping along to the ironmongers for a pound of nails or going along to the local decorators shop for some whitewash for the

cellar is no longer enough for today's discerning DIY enthusiast, nor for the 21st century's ambitious gardeners who now want water features as much as crocus bulbs. There is a plethora of DIY Stores and Garden Centres on the outskirts of every town, but who keeps these stores stocked with supplies? The answer in many cases is the largest and fastest growing DIY, hardware and gardening wholesaler in the region, Dompak Grosvenor, based in Widnes and now part of the even larger Stax group of companies. But Dompak wasn't always so large.

Domcraft Ltd, as the company was originally known, was founded in 1905 by two brothers, Jewish immigrants from Poland, Mo and Max Glassman who supplied cabinet makers with accessories, timber and handles etc. Mo however would leave the firm during the first word war to serve as a soldier; fortunately he returned unscathed.

For a while it looked as though the family firm would not have a second generation to run it as the brothers' two sons Harold and Irvine saw their future elsewhere: after serving an apprenticeship with English Electric Harold joined the army during the second world war before going into mining. Irvine actually trained to be a barrister before joining

*Top: A Domcraft monthly review from 1969. **Right:** The old Domcraft Ltd premises in Edwards Lane, Speke.*

the company (he would later put his legal training to good use by becoming a magistrate). Harold and Irvine Glassman continued the business which eventually changed direction to supply the emerging DIY market. Harold was company Chairman in charge of buying and sales whilst Irvine acted as Managing Director and concentrated on finance and administration.

In the 1960s, to meet the emerging DIY market, the firm had moved from its original location in Islington, Liverpool to much larger premises in Edwards Lane, Speke.

In April 1986 the business was sold on to a Scottish company, Walter Alexander PLC of Falkirk, whose main business was constructing body chassis for buses and trains. In 1991 however David Broudie, Michael Kneale and Michael Brown conducted a management buy-out. Sadly in 1997, due to a recession in the industry, the company went into liquidation threat-

ening redundancy for the 80 staff.

Fortunately the Stax company now rescued Domcraft and launched Dompak-Grosvenor Ltd a subsidiary of the Stax plc group as a wholesaler delivering goods to customers rather than selling on a cash and carry basis.

Stax is a non-food, cash and carry wholesaler strictly for the trade and specialises in DIY, hardware and gardening products. Customers are mainly independent retailers. Between 1988 and the start of the new century Stax would treble the number of its branches and more than quadruple its turnover, underlining its claim to be the most rapidly growing wholesaler in the country. But where did this extraordinarily dynamic company have its origins?

It was in 1981 that Stax Manchester began trading. By 1985 turnover had topped £4 million. The following year Eddie Brady and David Hibbert acquired the business, then owned by Maccess, in a management buy-out.

That may sound simple, but things were rather more complicated than that. The original Stax Trade Centre goes

back to a cash and carry wholesale business set up by Maccess the motor parts distributor back in 1981. Two Stax sites, Manchester and Leeds, opened that year.

Another branch opened in Tottenham, North London, in 1983. Despite increasing the range of goods sold to include bulk chemicals, catering equipment, ceramic

Top right: A company invoice from the 1970s.
Above left: David Hibbert and Eddie Brady, joint Managing Directors of Stax.
Left: The aftermath of the devastating fire at the Manchester branch of Stax that occurred in 1988.

non-executive director Graham Gardiner, negotiated a £750,000 buy out from Maccess which resulted in the formation of Stax Trade Centres Ltd.

Two years later Stax was able to open a Birmingham depot at Smethwick in the west Midlands. Within 12 months sales would top £10 million.

Having seen the original Leeds branch close in the 1980s Eddie and David now opened a new Leeds branch in 1992. Stax would go on to acquire its close rival WE Merris in Birmingham in 1995 and the following year the 52,000 sq ft Bristol branch of Stax would open.

tiles, furniture and office stationery the business however failed to thrive. All three sites were in the red and the decision was taken to close Tottenham in December 1994. The head office in Leeds was also closed leaving just two branches, each with a high degree of autonomy.

The Manchester branch was left to be run by Eddie Brady who had been the branch manager there since its opening in 1981. In 1984, on the closure of the Tottenham branch and subsequently the Leeds office, David Hibbert was transferred to Manchester to work with Eddie with the responsibility for negotiating business terms and marketing.

Under Eddie and David the Manchester branch began to flourish as they exercised their autonomy, pioneering what would become the well known Stax formula of keen pricing and regular promotions on a comprehensive range of products stocked in depth.

Despite that triumph in Manchester however the Leeds branch continued to lose money. Maccess took the decision to close the Leeds branch and Eddie and David took the chance to buy out the Manchester branch. In September 1986, Eddie and David, helped financially by

From a turnover of £2.5 million in 1981 sales had grown every single year, slowly at first reaching just £15 million in 1991 before rapidly taking off to reach that staggering £70 million at the start of the new millennium.

And it was not just sales that had grown. In the years since its founding staff numbers had increased from 50 to over 600. In 1987 the wages bill was £380,000, by 2000 it had reached £7.6 million. Staff who

Top left: An aerial view which shows the extent of Stax, Manchester, after the extension. **Above right:** *The launch of Stax, Bristol, 1996.* **Right:** *Part of the Dompak Show at Aintree.*

some multiple retailers too. The product range today is much more varied than in the past having moved on from just DIY products to include power tools, household goods, gardening products and pet accessories. The company is also focusing strongly on its own brand products including brass door furniture under the trade names of Woodside and Dompak. Products are sourced internationally though the company sells many famous brands such as Swish, Polycel and Cuprinol.

Within three years of being taken over Dompak turnover had grown from a standing start to £11 million and it now expects to continue to grow by acquisitions and organic growth - progress which the Glassman brothers would undoubtedly have been proud of.

joined the firm as general assistants on the shop floor could, with hard work and commitment, become senior managers within the group.

The growth of Stax has been remarkable, however nothing would have been possible without Eddie Brady and David Hibbert who bravely risked their all back in 1986.

Following the Stax rescue in 1997 Dompak leased an additional building on an industrial estate near the airport before moving to its present site on the Expressway Industrial estate at Widnes in 2001.

Today Dompak has 99 staff. The company concentrates on the wholesale market selling to independent retailers and

Top: The Dompak warehouse at Sky Park. **Above left:** *Some of the staff at the Dompak Show at Aintree, 1999.* **Right:** *David Broudie, Managing Director of Dompak Grosvenor Ltd.*

The sands of time

'Sand winning' will be an unfamiliar expression to anyone outside the specialised business of commercially extracting sand from both land and the sea. But people have been winning sand for thousands of years. It is one of the most basic building materials and was being used by the Romans as a critical ingredient of concrete even before the birth of Christ.

But not only is sand used for making concrete and cement, it is also an important component in many industrial applications such as making moulds for casting metal, for use in water filters and, perhaps most notably of all, as the main ingredient of glass. Without sand the world would be a very different place with no concrete to build motorway flyovers, no cast iron garden chairs and no glass for our greenhouses nor bottles to pour our wine from.

Though large deposits of sand can often be found far inland, as any boy or girl can tell you, the most likely place to look for sand in quantity is at the sea side. The commercial extraction or 'winning' of marine sand from this area has been on going for a very long time.

Today one of the most important companies involved in the sand winning trade is Liverpool's William Rainford (Holdings) Ltd along with its subsidiary, the Southport Sand Company Ltd.

William Rainford (Holdings) Ltd is a locally based business where plant and equipment is obtained through local dealerships that, together with servicing,

Top left: Founder, William Rainford.
Above: W Rainford invoice dated 1925.
Below: An early company service van.

maintenance and other purchases, annually amounts to over £3 million of spending in the Merseyside area.

Today the company is itself part of Thomas Armstrong (Holdings) Ltd which operates throughout the north of England.

At William Rainford (Holdings) Ltd the company has records dating back to 1925 relating to dealing in sand; an original quotation for sand from W Rainford of White Edge Farm, Hightown, with the telephone number 14 and dated 26 October, 1925, offers sand at two shillings a load - and one horse for 17 shillings and sixpence a day!

The present firm was formed by William 'Bill' Rainford and his two brothers, who eventually traded as William Rainford (Holdings) Ltd.

Around 1960 William Rainford bought the entire shareholding of the Southport Sand Company from its then owners, the Shearstone family.

During the years 1960 to 1975 the company was involved with demolition, coal and reclaimed building materials as well as sand. The transport fleet increased to over 200 vehicles of various types, including damp sand tippers, bulk cement and dried sand tankers and Readymix concrete mixer trucks and they had numerous Readymix concrete depots throughout the North West.

The 'A, B & C' licensed lorries connected to the old coal business were contracted to remove the ash from Chadderton, Penwortham and Clarence Dock power stations, and the firm also worked internally at Fiddlers Ferry transporting ash to the lagoons there.

The furnace bottom ash was transported from Clarence Dock and Penwortham power stations to Heysham Road, Aintree where William Rainford diversified into the manufacture of Breeze and concrete building blocks.

At the same time the Southport Sand Company also expanded with a drying plant at Crosby, sand-winning from the Royal Birkdale and Hillside Golf Clubs, Crosby, Birkdale and undertaking sand removal at Balls Hill to eliminate wind blown sand emanation on to the new Ainsdale coastal road. Gradually the company worked its way to Marshside and on to the constantly fed Horse Bank at Southport.

Bill Rainford was fully aware that if he could get across the Bog Hole onto this offshore sand bank the

Top: A birds eye view of W Rainford (Holdings) Ltd (left) and a company leaflet. Above left: Old W Rainford trucks. Left: Road building in the late 1950s, early 1960s.

business of Pilkington Glass at its Safety Glass Polishing Plant at Doncaster could be serviced and supplied with its needs. At Horse Bank sand and marshland accretion, dating back to the 1850s, is a well known fact in Southport, and this accretion was on top of the millions of tonnes of sand pumped back by dredgers into the Irish Sea each year to keep the estuary clear for shipping into Preston Docks.

The company had moved from Everton valley to its then brand new present offices in Heysham Road Aintree in 1967. In 1968 the dried sand business expanded, and a new 'Parker' drying plant was bought and erected at Heysham Road to replace the Crosby sand drying plant.

The following year saw even more investment. A new fully automatic block manufacturing plant was bought and installed at Heysham Road to replace the old and original 'egg laying' system of making building blocks. Today William Rainford and their subsidiary concrete block manufacturing company Barnetts (Buglawton) Ltd produce in the region of 15 million building blocks each year.

Despite these developments, or perhaps because of them, the mid 1970s saw the business split in two. In 1975 the Readymix concrete business and all the depots and mixer trucks were sold to Tarmac and with that area of the business went the associated workforce. This left William Rainford (Holdings) Ltd, including the Southport Sand Company, trading very much as it would be at the start of the new millennium.

By 1978 the company was looking for useful locations and extra sand winning opportunities within the Ribble estuary with the start of another marine sand winning operation off Salters Bank. This sand however, proved to be very fine and

would not meet neither Pilkington's nor any other industrial sand specification or have any other uses except for construction purposes compared to the sand from Horse Bank which the company had by then been winning for many years.

The entire shareholding of William Rainford (Holdings) was sold in 1995 to Thomas Armstrong (Holdings) Ltd a Cumbria based firm employing over 800 people. This new player was a private, well respected and professional firm and was trading both profitably and efficiently with an annual turnover of some £70 million.

Thomas Armstrong ranked as one of the oldest private businesses in West Cumbria having been set up in 1830 by the eponymous Thomas Armstrong, a joiner, cabinet maker and wheelwright, at 18 Main Street, Cockermouth.

From that small beginning Armstrong's business

*Top: Tip work in the early 1960s. **Above right:** The company's present 16 acre site at Heysham Road, Aintree. **Above:** The site of The Southport Sand Company, part of William Rainford (Holdings) Ltd.*

(Aggregates) Ltd and Thomas Armstrong (Construction) Ltd, these in addition to Washington Estates Ltd; The Lakes Homecentre Ltd; Barnetts (Buglawton) Ltd; Coulthard's Concrete Blocks (1980) Ltd and last but not least William Rainford (Holdings) Ltd and its subsidiaries.

Today the Southport Sand Company, part of William Rainford (Holdings) Ltd is a very small firm, basically one man and his digger, but it has a very significant part to play in the manufacture of wired safety glass for use in schools, hospitals and public places; this glass is polished with Southport sand and exported to over 50 countries throughout the world, including the USA.

For more than three quarters of a century the name of William Rainford has been associated with winning sand. Today that name and that long tradition of winning sand from both land and sea continue unabated. From its base in Aintree the company not only employs large numbers of staff but it generates many more jobs through its deliberate policy of buying plant and equipment through local dealers. And wherever Liverpudlians travel in the world the chances are high that, thanks to William Rainford, they will see those far off views through a sheet of glass made from sand won from our very own off shore sand bank in the Mersey estuary.

continued to expand, although by 1929 the founder's family had withdrawn its interests and in 1930 Thomas Armstrong Ltd was registered as a limited company. The second world war brought about a tremendous upsurge in demand for timber and Thomas Armstrong Ltd's employees felled and processed for many years areas of standing timber in and around Cumbria.

In the post war years the Cumbrian company took advantage of the demand in the North East for rebuilding of the bombed areas of Newcastle and Sunderland, opening a Thomas Armstrong branch in Newcastle in 1946. It was also around that time that the company began to manufacture concrete blocks and, in particular, patented its Clinecon Block, an interlocking building block which speeded up the building of homes - over 10,000 Clinecon block built houses are in existence.

By the end of the 20th century the Thomas Armstrong group of companies owned by Thomas Armstrong (Holdings) Ltd would comprise no fewer than five companies bearing the Thomas Armstrong name: Thomas Armstrong (Concrete Blocks) Ltd; Thomas Armstrong (Timber) Ltd; Thomas Armstrong

Top and above left: A tanker and trucks from the company's present fleet. Below: William Rainford (Holdings) Ltd offices in Heysham Road, Aintree.

Better homes

Slowly but surely the worst of the City's old unsatisfactory housing has disappeared or been renovated. Much of that work is down to Housing Associations.

Liver Housing Association was formed in 1966 when a group of professionals came together to help provide quality rented housing at a time of great shortage. The key people involved were Peter Jones of Venmore Thomas and Jones (surveyors and estate agents), Lawrence Jones of Thomas R Jones and Sons (solicitors), Mr R Black of Page, Burne and Black (accountants), Alex Burdekin, of the National Westminster Bank in the Fruit Exchange and Richard Crawshaw, a local MP. Since its formation the Association has played an important role working in partnership with Liverpool City Council and the Housing Corporation (a government agency) providing affordable homes in Merseyside for people in need. Throughout it's existence Liver was successful in its work to build and improve homes through the coupling of its social aims and the forward looking vision of the Association's board of unpaid volunteers.

One of the Association's first developments, 'Sunnyside', is situated off Devonshire Road and forms a small secluded cul-de-sac on the edge of Princes Park. The majority of houses in Sunnyside are owned by Housing Association's, Liver being one, though two houses are privately owned whilst another is a nursing home. There have been houses in Sunnyside since the latter part of the 19th century when Liverpool was enjoying the wealth created by its links with the colonies and North America. The buildings in Sunnyside therefore form an important part of Liverpool's architectural heritage and because of that, Sunnyside, and the surrounding area, are part of the Princes Park Conservation Area. It was during the early 1980s that the Association recognised that its older residents, those which it had housed during the 60s and 70s, might one day need sheltered accommodation. With that

Above, both pictures: Liver property on Canning Street both before and after renovation.
Below: Tenement buildings in Old Swan during clearance in the mid 1990s.

in mind the Association enlarged its existing role to create Livercare to help in providing accommodation with care and support for the frail elderly. By 1996 the Association would have six homes with well trained staff, homes about which Social Services inspectors would consistently report on the excellence of the care to be found there.

By the by the end of its first quarter century of existence it was receiving annual income in rents of almost £6 million, some £2.3 million of which was being reapplied to repairs and maintenance of property.

In the intervening years much had been achieved: in 1989 for example Liver acquired 700 properties on the Brookvale Estate in Runcorn. In the following three years tenants, owner occupiers and staff would see numerous changes, not least a major programme of repairs whilst dealing with 'environmental issues such as the upkeep of the estate's landscaped areas tree-felling and re-planting. Over the next year the Association would also buy properties in the Runcorn Old Town, Widnes and Brookvale to provide much needed accommodation. Elsewhere, in Kirby, Liver, together with three other Associations participated in the Kirby Initiative which involved the conversion of a range of new and refurbished homes whilst in Widnes

Top left: An aerial view of the plaza in front of the Anglican Cathedral during the development of Liver's Cathedral Mews and Alfred Mews (circa 1990). ***Right:*** The peaceful setting of Moorehaven Residential Home which closed when it didn't meet new Government standards.

Madeleine McKenna Court was officially opened in July 1992, accommodation which provided a 22 bed residential home for the frail elderly together with 11 bungalows connected by intercom to the home.

That year the Association moved to new offices in Columbus Quay away from its old Victoria Street offices which had been too small and suffered from poor access. The following year, 1993, saw the transfer of all Livercare's tenancies back to Liver Housing due to reorganisation within the Liver Housing Group, a change which enabled the Liver Group to provide a much more cost-effective and efficient service in the future.

Liver reached a major milestone in 1994 when it completed its 4,000th 'housing unit' since its beginnings in 1966. To mark the occasion Anthony Mayer the Chief Executive of the Housing Corporation drove a jeep through a giant paper banner proclaiming the fact that this incredible target had been reached. Also present was 11 year old Lee Burns winner of a competition to find a name for the access road to the development where the 4,000th home had been completed, consequently named Cherrybank. That same year Environment Minister Robert Jones announced a £1 million contribution towards the cost of redeveloping Gleave Square. It would be supplemented by £1.5 million raised by Liver Housing which had been responsible for co-ordinating the scheme from the start. The funding meant a huge boost for much-needed rented accommodation in the area, particularly since it included a promise of major funding package for 150 houses to be built in Huyton and Kirby.

It is however perhaps in property rehabilitation that the Association has made its greatest impact. There is a long history of street rehabilitation throughout Merseyside rooted in the problems associated with private housing which is mainly of pre-1919 vintage. The situation was recognised in the late 1970s when the Housing Corporation invested substantial amounts of money in rehabilitation. That funding was linked to Housing Action Area Programmes; in such designated areas local authorities

would offer landlords discretionary improvement grants, whilst compulsorily purchasing those properties which had not been improved within the statutory time limit. Such purchases were then vested in Housing Associations for them to make improvements. Though improvement grants would eventually become a thing of the past Liver would continue to use rehabilitation as a way of addressing each area's housing problems. In fact, out of Liver's total stock, almost 1700 homes would be rehabilitation projects, the majority being in Liverpool 4, 5 and 6. The last portfolio of properties to be acquired following compulsory purchase was in the Rockfield Road Housing action area in July 1994, a portfolio which contained 21 homes.

By the mid 1990s progress was accelerating. In 1995/96 the Association was able to hand over 266 homes to people in housing

Top: May Place the Liver's sheltered scheme on Broadgreen Road. Formerly St Vincent's Hospice. Inset: May Place circa 1923. Above: Mosslake, apartments built for shared ownership sale on the site of the former Catholic Apostolic Church on the corner of Canning Street and Catherine Street.

need and begin work on another 303 in Liverpool, Sefton, Knowsley, Halton and Wirral. The Association collaborated with local authorities, agencies and tenants to improve, adapt and build homes to the highest standard. In Gleave Square the Association replaced damp and vandalised deck-access blocks with an estate of houses and bungalows with gardens. In Sefton the Association worked with Bootle Maritime City Challenge to produce 41 new homes by Strand Road and began the regeneration of Bootle Village. In Rock Ferry a hard-to-let property was converted into accommodation for use by young single mothers and women at risk, whilst for people with disabilities the Association installed showers and stair lifts in properties whilst providing support and advice to tenants' groups.

In the Old Swan district of Liverpool the tenements at St Oswald's House, St Oswald Gardens and Hurst Gardens were in a serious state of disrepair. The buildings had been erected by the city council just before and immediately after the war. A total of 112 homes would be built in Old Swan as part of Project Orchid. One key element was the redevelopment of St Vincent's Hospice on Broadgreen Road where Liver's

sheltered housing scheme, May Place, was created whilst still preserving the the facade of this Grade II listed building. The Liver Association raised £3.53 million of the total £6.4 million of the overall scheme.

The Association had become prominent in the regeneration of Liverpool, not least by participating in City Challenge. The aim of City Challenge would be to regenerate specific areas by top slicing various government department budgets whilst taking a focused approach which crossed departmental boundaries. A major feature of such schemes is the emphasis placed on working closely with local communities for the benefit of all. Liver would be particularly active in assisting in the regeneration of Canning, the largest area of Georgian housing in the North West of England, the association being awarded the task of acquiring and improving a number of listed buildings. By working in partnership with the Housing Corporation, Liverpool City Challenge, the City Council and English Heritage, Liver would rise to the challenge. As

a result the Association was able to acquire three properties for conversion into flats at affordable rents. Properties in Canning Street, for example, were acquired from Liverpool City Council in a dilapidated condition and would undergo complete refurbishment, the cost being met by Housing Association grant and private borrowing whilst other costs were met by English Heritage.

In the same period the Association would work closely with Bootle Maritime City Challenge to complete 41 more new houses on sites adjoining Strand Road in the former 'Tree Streets' Housing Action Area. As Liver's first 'Green Scheme' particular care would be taken to fulfil the City Challenge request to consider environmental issues. The project would be used as an example for others to follow.

New directions

In August 2001 Liver merged with St Helens based Grosvenor Housing Association. As a result of the merger, which was fully supported by residents, Liver changed its name to Arena Housing Association. The new association which owns 11,000 homes continues Liver's good work but with the advantage of greater financial resources to invest in homes and communities.

And please keep your eyes peeled - the Liver's good work is still continuing through its successor, Arena Housing Association.

__Above left:__ Bootle Village (you will notice the Inland Revenue office block in the background that has now been demolished). __Above right:__ Making people happy through Liver's work on the Kirby strategy in the mid 1990s. __Left:__ Residents looking at Liver's plans for new homes and bungalows built to replace the horrific deck access flats at Gleave Square, Everton Road. The new estate has been re-named Everton Gardens.

Bricks and mortar-
The Venmore Partnership

There cannot be many readers who can remember when you could buy a five bedroom house in Liverpool for £150; but the records of one Liverpool firm show that it was quite possible back in 1920.

The Venmore Partnership - Venmore, Thomas & Jones and Ball & Percival is a team of highly experienced professionals whose roots go back more than a century and a half; today the partnership provides a complete range of property services throughout Merseyside and West Lancashire from its seven offices around Liverpool, Kirkby, Southport and Tarleton.

Thomas & Jones was founded in the 1890s. The founding partners, Messrs Thomas and Jones, were estate agents in the original meaning of the words - they managed rows of terraced houses which were let on weekly tenancies; they collected the rent, organised repairs, dealt with

re-letting and acted usually on behalf of others, though sometimes they were landlords themselves.

The two founders were both Welsh and they capitalised on this by acting for the many Welsh builders who were active in Liverpool at that time.

Mr Thomas left the firm within three or four years of its foundation, but his partner Mr Jones, continued to expand the business. During the inter war years he took his son into the business but the association did not last long. In the 1930s a Mr Russell acquired the business and after the second world war he took into partnership a Mr Lloyd-Jones.

Mr Russell retired in the mid 1950s and Peter Jones began with the firm as an assistant in 1959. Soon afterwards Mr Lloyd-Jones died very suddenly and for some time the business was run by Peter Jones and the office manager George Morgan on behalf of Lloyd-Jones' widow; before long, however, Peter Jones and George Morgan bought the business.

The firm continued to expand, mainly by providing valuation and survey services to Building Societies; at this time, 1960, Mike Earl joined the business as an assistant.

In the 1960s several small property management businesses were acquired by Thomas & Jones as well as the business of Herbert Davies in Birkenhead. That acquisition took the firm into a new area of business, design work, usually for local builders, and also into a very profitable though short-lived period when the firm purchased land on behalf of both small and large builders.

Top: James Venmore, founder partner of W&J Venmore.
Left: An advertisement for Ball and Percival, 1900.

George Morgan retired in 1973 four years after Mike Earl had become a partner. By that time Peter Jones had, together with an accountant and a solicitor, founded the Liver Housing Association. Thomas & Jones carried out a considerable amount of work for the Association including the acquisition, design, conversion and upgrading of property, followed by its management on behalf of the Association. Eventually, however, the government decided that it was best if housing associations were independent of their professional advisers though by this time Liver Housing Association had a portfolio of nearly 800 properties.

In 1976 Thomas & Jones acquired the practice known as Patterson & Thomas and for a few happy years David Jones, from that firm, joined the partnership. Patterson & Thomas was one of the oldest firms in Liverpool having been founded in 1849. For much of that time it had occupied the Grade One listed building at 16 Cook Street. Thomas & Jones were next door at number 14 and so a bridge was built between the two buildings. The merger meant that Thomas & Jones now included commercial property work as part of the practice with David Jones; for a short time he and David Inman dealt with this part of the business. David Inman however only stayed for two or three years before going abroad to work. Meanwhile the survey business had expanded and Derek Coates joined as a partner in the mid 1970s. Auction sales of property were also carried out, this having been a regular part of Thomas & Jones activities since the firm's foundation.

Elsewhere in the firm the Drawing Office and Building Surveying side had grown from its tiny start which had begun with the purchase, years earlier, of Herbert

Davies and now had a partner and four technicians fully occupied. However, that side of the business would split away from Thomas & Jones in the 1980s and lead to the formation of the firm of Taylor Hutchinson.

It was in the 1980s that a lengthy period of discussion with the firm of W&J Venmore led to the eventual amalgamation of the two firms and to the new firm of Venmore, Thomas & Jones.

W&J Venmore took its name from twin brothers, William and James Venmore, sons of the High Sheriff of Anglesey; they had come from Llannerch-y-medd as young men in the late 19th century and established an estate agents business with offices in Liverpool's Scotland Road. James also became a J.P. and High Sheriff of Anglesey.

James Venmore's sons Arthur and Cecil would carry on the family business after the deaths of their father and uncle, who curiously died within eight hours of one another in December 1920.

Arthur and Cecil Venmore were joined in 1936 by C Roger Morton. Arthur and Cecil Venmore died in 1961 and 1974 respectively. Roger who was awarded the VC during the war ran the partnership with the third generation of the Venmore family, Neville Venmore, until Neville's death in 1972; Miles Pickering then joined the firm which went from strength to strength as a result of Roger's deep

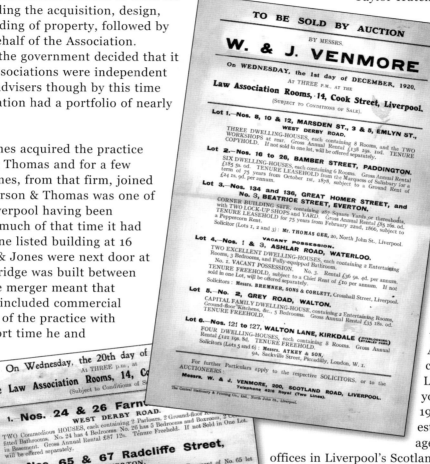

This page: Lots for auction in the 1920s.

local knowledge of people, properties, and the professional experience gained by Miles. It was following Roger's retirement that, due to the size of the firm, Miles Pickering had to seek assistance from others which in turn resulted in the amalgamation with Thomas & Jones - a very similar professional firm.

Meanwhile in Southport the firm of Ball & Percival had been established in June 1900 by Walter Knight Ball and a Mr Percival. The partnership split up in the early days leaving Walter Ball on his own. An advert in a local newspaper for September 1900 refers to Walter having previously had 11 years experience with a firm called Hindle & Son and the new business was established as a firm of Auctioneers, Valuers, Estate and Insurance Agents, Mortgage Brokers and Accountants with offices at St George's Place 138d Lord Street, Southport.

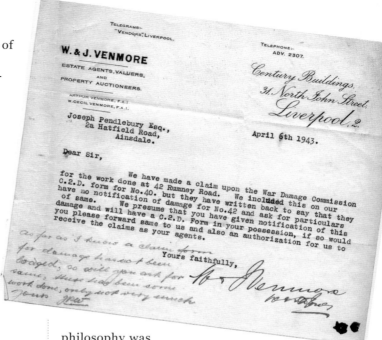

The business relocated in 1905 to premises it still occupies, next door to the General Post Office at 132 Lord Street; a substantially larger building with office accommodation on four floors.

One of Walter Ball's sons, Raymond Knight Ball took over the firm on his father's retirement early in the 1930s and in the 1940s the first non-family members became partners. Raymond Ball retired in 1964 a year after Bruce Jones joined the firm. The firm continued to prosper as an independent partnership until August 1986 when it became a limited liability company and was taken over by Hambro Countrywide Plc, the largest estate agency chain in the United Kingdom. Hambro's initial philosophy was to retain local established trading names and the business, now a division of Hambro, continued to trade as Ball & Percival. In 1988 however there was a name change followed by a subsequent decline in the business which was by then operating from five more offices at Tarleton, Ainsdale, Formby, Ormskirk and Burscough - plus a short-lived seventh office in Crosby.

Bruce Jones resigned his directorship on the change of name at the end of 1988; with a business colleague he established a niche property consultancy; he subsequently bought back the professional side of the former Ball & Percival business at the beginning of 1990 trading from 21 Hoghton Street in Southport. But that was far from the end of the story.

In mid 1991 Bruce Jones was concerned to see his former business in even further decline and despite still occupying its four storey building it was only utilising the ground floor. It was becoming obvious that within a few years this division of Hambro

Top right: A letter dated April 1943 from W. & J. Venmore acting as agents for a claim upon the War Damage Commission. **Above:** Old and modern 'To Let' and 'For Sale' signs. **Left:** Details for the auction of numbers 1 to 65 Anglesey Street, Bootle in 1923.

Countryside would virtually cease to exist having during the interim period already closed four of its local offices.

A buy back of what was left of the business was negotiated with the deal being concluded in November 1991; at the same time Ball & Percival now led by Bruce Jones merged with the even longer established practice of Venmore Thomas & Jones in Liverpool.

In 1999 Philip Cassidy joined the Partnership and, as a result, has been able to enhance an already successful auction department. The six-weekly auctions result in sales in excess of one thousand properties per annum. In 2000 Simon Wall joined the Partnership and is now Managing Partner with Miles Pickering as Senior Partner.

The Partners are also Directors of Colette Gunter Ltd, Formby's most experienced Estate Agents and Venmore Thomas and Jones (Prescot) Ltd with offices in St Helens, Prescot and Newton-le Willows under the Management of Michael Murphy.

Today, though it is no longer possible to buy a house for £150, the Venmore Partnership still endeavours to give its clients as good a service now as they might have received at any time in the last 150 years.

Above left: The Venmore Partnership's longest-standing Partner, Mike Earl, who in 2002 retired after more than forty years service with the firm.
Right: Miles Pickering gaining entry to Kemlyn Road - the last house to be vacated prior to their client, Liverpool Football Club, building the Centenary Stand on the site. *Below:* The firm's Lord Street, Southport, office.

Windows of opportunity

Fenestration; there's a word to conjure with. A dictionary definition relates to it meaning the arrangement of windows in a building. A Liverpool company, which knows all there is to know about fenestration, is Rea Metal Windows Limited. The company has been in the business of manufacturing, installing and glazing window frames since the reign of Edward VII.

Rea Metal Windows Limited was founded by Daniel Arthur Rea, a Liverpool businessman, who in 1906 purchased a disused Rice Mill in Etna Street, off Green Lane, in Liverpool 13, for the purpose of manufacturing steel window frames (then known as casements) and leaded lights. Perhaps the founder had been inspired to start this business by one of the greatest architectural and engineering feats of the Victorian age, the creation of the Crystal Palace - then still standing - a massive iron and glass structure which had originally housed Prince Albert's Exhibition many decades earlier. If we cannot be certain what first inspired Daniel Rea, he certainly knew a good thing when he saw it. He recognised the aesthetic advantage of slim sight lines with inherent strength that steel window frames had over the main competition of wooden frames.

The new company specialised in purpose made windows mainly for commercial buildings, schools, hospitals, churches and prisons. The mass produced, standard sized, windows used mainly in the housing sector were not considered commercially viable for the scale of operation being run by Rea Metal Windows. The same general policy of manufacturing purpose made windows is still in place today, however, there is an increasing market for the product in existing buildings being refurbished and subject to a change of use from commercial and industrial to residential.

The early years of the company saw steady progress and the labour force increased from ten to eighteen as the company's

Right: *Welding by hand.*
Below: *The workforce pictured at the start of the 20th century.*

In the period between the two world wars, the company undertook the steel window installation in the Bon Marche and Lewis' stores. After the Second World War, those were followed by Marks and Spencer's and most recently by the Littlewoods store, both in Church Street. The redevelopment of the old Bryant and May factory in Speke (now known as 'The Matchworks') and the refurbishment of one of the hangars at the site of the original Liverpool Airport, are amongst the more prominent local contracts recently completed. Perhaps the most interesting involvement Rea Metal Windows has had with a prominent local building is with The Blackburn Assurance Company Building in Dale Street, adjacent to the Queensway Mersey Tunnel entrance. The company installed the original windows in 1934 and the replacement windows when the building was refurbished in 2000.

An extensive export market was developed between the wars and many large buildings in China, Egypt, India, and South Africa - amongst other countries - were supplied with Rea's purpose made windows. The advent of war in 1939 put a close to the export market and the firm switched to vital armament work for the Admiralty. One of the more unusual products made by the company were large airtight steel tanks about the

hand made products were installed in a number of notable buildings throughout the United Kingdom.

The production process in the 4 storey rice mill required that the bars of steel be hoisted to the top floor, before being cut to size by hand with hacksaws. Holes were formed in the bars by small punching and drilling machines before the bars. were welded into frames. The earliest frames were made from wrought iron, followed later by steel and occasionally brass would be used, although this was too expensive for most clients and eventually demand petered out. Prior to the second world war, the steel frames would be given a coat of red oxide paint before being despatched. Post 1945 new rustproofing methods were introduced first in the form of zinc metal spraying, later hot dip galvanising. In the 1960s the firm began experimenting with colour finishing processes, initially sintered nylon granules, then in the 1970s fused polyester powders, applied over the galvanised surface, were introduced and have become the standard finish for most of the products.

Top left: New windows at 'The Matchworks'.
Top right: Liverpool's John Moore University.
***Above left:** A craftsman at work. **Right**: The extensive storeroom.*

size of a modern living room; these were coupled together at sea to form the base for a floating roadway, later known as the Mulberry Harbours, to be used by the allied invasion forces.

Following the end of the Second World War in 1945, the company expanded its manufacturing facilities with new plant, machinery and buildings and began to carry out numerous projects in the government's enormous school building programme. Steel windows were particularly popular at this time because the import of timber was restricted; this led to a massive increase in the use of steel window frames for all types of building.

A factory was started in Belfast and produced steel windows mainly for school buildings in Northern Ireland. Production ceased a few years later when the building was destroyed by fire. The expanded production facility in Liverpool made it possible to carry out the Northern Ireland contracts and it was decided not to restart production in Belfast

There was a progressive decline in the whole industry during the late 1970s to early 1990s due to the introduction of alternative framing materials, first aluminium and subsequently uPVC. These materials had certain advantages in that they required lower capital outlay for machinery and fewer processes to produce a finished product. The result was that more companies came into the purpose made window market and competition drove down prices. Rea Metal Windows decided not to follow the trend to produce windows from the new materials. In the long run, this proved to be the correct decision because many long established companies who did make the transition to the new materials found that there was insufficient profit to sustain their existence.

A resurgence in the product started in the early 1990s, attributable to two main factors. There was a growing trend starting in London, for old warehouse buildings to be converted into inner city apartments. Most of these would have had either cast iron or wrought iron window frames. The modern steel window was the nearest available product in keeping with the original material and planning approvals tended to require the use of the closest matching product. Secondly, architects who had been at school and students during the main years of the steel window's decline became aware of the main advantages of the strength of steel framing within slender sight lines and the ability of the product to be formed into tight radiused curved shapes.

The younger architects started to take advantage of these attributes within new building designs. At this point in time there had been a large reduction in the number of companies

Top right: Bill Johnson pointing to circular frames.
Above: A general view of the factory. Left: The re-windowed Blackburn Assurance Building.

offering the production capacity and expertise, so who better for them to contact than Rea Metal Windows.

The company's founder Daniel Rea retired in 1932 and the company suffered financially during the depression. Recovery began and was sustained when Mr W E Johnson became Managing Director during the war and subsequently Chairman in 1984. He retired in 1994 after serving with the company continuously for 66 years, having started out as the office boy straight from St Anne's School, Stanley in 1928. He is now the Honorary President and at the start of the 21st Century is still being consulted on matters of detail, custom and practice relating to the company and industry from a time years before anyone else was around.

The Johnson name, however, remained central to Rea Metal Windows: Eddie Johnson joined the company in 1965 and Peter Johnson in 1979. It was Peter who succeeded his father in 1984 as Managing Director and subsequently as Chairman ten years later.

Peter introduced a policy of striving for industry wide recognised quality standards and saw the company awarded the first British Standard Kitemark for a range of steel windows. The company was selected as an approved supplier and installer of windows for the Property Services Agency of the government, who were responsible for maintaining government owned buildings and establishments, for three successive three year periods, until the demise of the PSA during the Thatcher years. Marketing opportunities in the European Union were explored and are being developed. A property of steel fire resistance, was taken on board when a range of fire resisting profiles were introduced that enabled the company to supplement its core production with products that met the exacting standards relating to fire and heat resistant framing and glazing. The increasingly high standards of thermal insulation required in new construction necessitated the design and development of a new range of profiles, which Peter undertook for the industry.

While all this was going on the company was gaining financial strength to the extent that Peter Johnson recommended to the Board of Directors that Rea Metal Windows buy out a rival business in Birmingham, which it duly did. Over a number of years both companies supplied and installed the steel windows in the Albert Dock buildings. Windows were also fitted in the Natural History Museum in Kensington, London. Other prestigious projects have included fire resisting doors to the Tate of the North Gallery in Liverpool, a new laboratory block at London's Great Ormond Street Childrens Hospital and the College Hall complex at RAF Cranwell.

After nearly a century of continuous trading the company is still making purpose made steel windows in the same place in which business began in 1906, although the workforce and buildings are, of course, larger. The constantly changing challenges of the market place and the striving to maintain the high standards of quality required to remain successful continue to be at the forefront of the endeavours of everyone associated with the company, where it has been well proven that 'quality breeds success'.

Above left: *Apartments on Liverpool's waterfront.*
Left: *Apartments on Tithebarn Street.*

The cutting edge

The world of computing is not one that immediately springs to mind when dealing with nostalgia, and yet what is still at the very cutting edge of modernity has been with us now for several decades. Although a mechanical forerunner of the computer, Charles Babbage's analytical engine, was designed in Victorian times, the modern electronic computer owes its origins to the top secret work of British code-breakers in the dark days of the second world war. By the 1960s what now seems like primitive technology was finding its way into the world of business. Those who were involved with computing in that period will recall punched paper tape and punched cards being used alongside massive reels of magnetic tapes.

But the history of hardware is not the whole story of computing. A computer on its own is nothing more than a useless box of electronics; what makes a computer valuable is what it is used for. Whilst some companies sold hardware others were busy helping clients discover how to use the new technology to make their businesses more effective.

Below: Founders of the Fraser Williams Group, Eric Williams, left and Tom McCafferty, right.

One such firm which entered that emerging services market with perfect timing was Liverpool based Fraser Williams Group.

FWL Technologies Ltd - the trading business of Fraser Williams Group, with its HQ in the old Port of Liverpool Building on the Pierhead, combines industry expertise, IT skills and specialist application packages to provide customers around the world with solutions in key areas of logistics, warehousing, shipping, freight, transport and finance.

Tom McCafferty, who along with Eric Williams founded the Fraser Williams Group, was born in Edgware, North London and gained a law degree from Bristol University before settling in Merseyside at the age of 27. At the age of 31 Tom quit his job as a computer services salesman for ICL. In just four years at ICL Tom had been promoted to management level with a company car but he was fed up with being stuck in an office and believed that there were major opportunities for newcomers in the still fledgling Information Technology industry.

At the time the South East of England had 99.5 per cent of all computer business but Tom and Eric

realised that demand would soon grow in the rest of Britain.

Together and with the investment of Duncan C Fraser & Co, who gave their name to the company Tom and Eric decided to exploit the demand for Information Technology services beyond London. And not just in the UK.

Few companies could ever rival Fraser Williams for the prestigious location of its first overseas contract in 1970. The client was Olympic Maritime, the Onassis shipping empire based in Monaco.

Running up to decimalisation in February 1971 the demise of the halfpenny, the half-crown and shilling was a fillip for the computer services industry and business boomed. That boom was however merely a prelude to the recession of 1971 and many companies disappeared over night. In deep trouble itself, with a trading loss of £30,000 set against a similar sized profit the previous year, Fraser William's hung on and with the help of loyal staff and clients survived its one major crisis.

*Top left: The co-founders pictured outside the Port of Liverpool building when the firm moved there in 1977. **Right:** A contract signing ceremony at Europa Transport.*

In the mid 1970s, around the time oil was first discovered in the North Sea, business was once again growing stronger at home and abroad and the company won major contracts in Nigeria and the Middle East. It was though only in the second half of the 1970s that things really began to take off.

On January 21st 1976 Concorde became the first and only plane to enter the supersonic passenger market. For Fraser Williams the pace of advancements in technology also quickened. More and more regional offices were established as the company continued to pioneer the concept of 'national strength, local service'. Turnover soon passed the million pound mark and from a position of loss in 1971 profits began to soar. Prestigious clients pointed the way for rapid growth in a variety of sectors.

Wimbledon's centenary year of 1977, in which Britain's Virginia Wade celebrated in style by winning the Ladies Singles title, also saw Fraser Williams make its first overseas acquisition: Buckley & Kelling in Toronto which would become Buckley Fraser Williams, one of three overseas subsidiaries.

Whilst viewers in the UK were getting their first glimpse of a new television series called Dallas, Fraser Williams was moving into its prestigious offices in the magnificent Port of Liverpool Building.

The marriage of Prince Charles to Lady Diana Spencer in 1981 was watched by 750 million people across the globe. But as one marriage began another ended when

IN GREAT WATERS

the company's relationship with its original backers became unnecessary. The parting was amicable with Fraser Williams being financially restructured as a management owned company in March 1981 with the financial assistance of 3i.

Group results for 1983/84 were cause for further celebration as net assets for the first time exceeded one million pounds - an indication of the company's stability enhanced by the spread of regional autonomous profit centres.

Two years later the company moved into Europe with the acquisition of Info Engineering in the Netherlands, a company which would in turn make two further acquisitions of its own. Also in 1986 Fraser Williams' innovative advertising monitoring service, Adtrack, won the Queen's Award for Exports.

By 1988 profits exceeded one million pounds, profits which were used to finance further growth and to develop new opportunities that fast evolving technologies were continually creating. Equally important however to the company was the investment in its people.

From its small start the Fraser Williams Group would grow to a conglomerate of IT Solutions companies. Over time the group rationalised its operations into specific market segments with member companies dedicated to sectors such as Supply Chain, Pharmaceuticals and Property Management. Within the group each company would enjoy a high level of autonomy whilst sharing central group resources.

Top: The Management team in 2002, from left - Dave Renshaw, Chief Operating Officer, Neil Garland, Chief Executive Officer and Malcolm Wright, Chief Financial Officer. Above: The Port of Liverpool Building at Pierhead, the firm's headquarters.

It was against this background that a Management Buy Out was instigated in 2002 with the existing management team of Neil Garland, Malcolm Wright, both born and bred in Liverpool, and Dave Renshaw, a Yorkshireman, buying the business from its founders.

Each of the team had spent more the 20 years in the business servicing such well known local clients as Exel, with its roots in Liverpool and the Ocean Steamship Company, alongside other Liverpool based customers such as Nightfreight, Harrison Line, Bibby Distribution, and Park Food Group.

By 1999, after 30 years of activity, the business would boast an annual turnover of £34 million with subsidiaries in the USA, Hong Kong, and the Netherlands in addition to a presence in Portugal and the Middle East with overseas sales accounting for a third of turnover.

Employing 700 people world wide, divestment and rationalisation would now take place - four group members FW Netherlands, Data Systems, Pharma Systems and Commercial Systems being sold between 1999 and 2001 whilst other group companies - Fraser Williams Manchester and Fraser Williams Financial Systems - would be absorbed into FWL Technologies Ltd, the most significant operation in the group. FWL Technologies would also acquire four other companies: Quintech bought in 1999 to address the special needs of publishing and media distribution and, in 2000, Anchor Marine for its ship and port solutions. In 2002 FWL Technologies acquired i-scope an internet based product in the USA. This acquisition places FWL at the cutting edge of information technology in the supply chain sector. The business has also acquired a software development centre near Mumboi, India.

After its reorganisations the company would employ a total team of some 400 people, only 40 of whom were based overseas, but an astonishing 244 of whom would be employed in product development. More than £5 million was spent on 'R&D' in the first three years of the new structure leading to an annual turnover of more than £17 million with customer sites in some 40 different countries from Seattle to Shanghai and from Latvia to Johannesburg.

In 2002 FWL Software released the most functional global supply chain solution covering the internet to the back office for organisations in shipping, freight forwarding, transport and distribution.

From humble beginnings FWL has grown a business that is able to meet the needs and aspirations of its customers wherever they may be in the world - whilst still remaining committed to its well established roots in Liverpool.

Top left: *Malcolm Wright.* ***Above right:*** *Dave Renshaw.* ***Below:*** *Neil Garland, Chief Executive Officer.*

New homes for old

It's getting harder every day to recall now just how tired and run down some of our cityscape looked 30 or 40 years ago. The building booms of the late Victorian period and early Edwardian times was long over; even homes built between the wars were beginning to look old and in many parts of the City leaking roofs and peeling paint were the all too visible legacy of their long neglect. Neither private landlords nor the City council had been able to do much to halt the decline; Herr Hitler's bombing had not done much to help either. After the end of the second world war building materials remained rationed for a long period and even when such restrictions were lifted neither the will nor the money seemed available to do anything about housing conditions in some of the worst parts of Liverpool.

Not that those who lived in run down areas of the City were necessary unhappy. We may have been poor but there wasn't much crime in those days when they said you could go away for a week and leave your front door unlocked and all would be fine when you returned. The cynics may say that was because we had nothing worth taking; but times were more secure. And we all remember the man who was asked whether it was safe not to have a lock on the door of his outdoor lavatory and nonchalantly replied that it had been like that for the last twenty years and nothing had been stolen so far!

Happy days indeed, but hard ones too, not least in Winter

with many trying to keep warm in damp sub-standard homes heated only by a single coal fire.

Since that time many older buildings have been demolished to make way for the new. More recently greater emphasis has been placed on refurbishing older buildings to grant them a new lease of life, bringing them up to modern standards whilst preserving their architectural merits. That process has occurred all over Britain but has been especially noticeable in Liverpool.

The Liverpool Housing Trust - LHT - was formed in 1965 at a time when housing problems had grown to crisis proportions. At that time the Trust was made up of a small group of local people who were determined to help house homeless families, particularly those in Liverpool 8.

Launched on a shoestring, and dependent upon the voluntary work of Committee members, from its first offices in Falkner Square the Trust began a fund-raising campaign to buy and improve older houses. It took three years to house the first five families, but then the vital financial support came from Shelter and the local council. The result was substantial growth, by 1970 the Trust's

This page: Examples of poor housing conditions.

staff numbered just six though by then they were managing 300 homes, and by 1973 the Trust had over 700 homes in its ownership.

In 1969 LHT helped set up the Shelter Neighbourhood Action Project in Granby, Liverpool 8, centred on one of the country's first General Improvement Areas and aimed at tackling the problems of neighbourhood decay. The three year project and its final report showed both the potential for improving areas of poor housing and the need for concerted and co-ordinated action.

The pioneering work of LHT and other Shelter sponsored housing associations over this period had a crucial impact on Government plans and the 1974 Housing Act, with all party support, introduced secure and comprehensive funding for housing associations. The Act also established the Housing Corporation, which monitors housing associations in its modern form. Further rapid growth followed with whole portfolios of housing being bought from Liverpool landlords to be improved for the benefit of tenants.

In 1976 Liverpool City Council changed its housing policy from large-scale clearance and redevelopment to area-based renewal by improvement. The success of LHT and others encouraged the City to give associations a lead role in the 53 Housing Action Areas declared in the following years. The work of area improvements would be central to the work of LHT in Liverpool from 1976. The result would be substantial concentrations of Trust ownership in Walton, Anfield, Granby and Garston.

As well as improving these mainly terraced family houses LHT would become involved in providing a wide range of housing types. These would include newbuild family housing, sheltered housing for the elderly, short-stay furnished flats for the homeless, mother and baby homes for young single parents, a refuge for children at risk, purpose built housing for the disabled, hostel housing for young ex-offenders and a substantial programme of intensively supported group homes for mentally handicapped and mentally ill adults.

Growth continued, by 1980 over 100 staff managed 3,000 homes. Today, 230 staff manage an astonishing 10,000 homes.

As the Liverpool Housing Trust grew a series of district offices would be set up to provide local housing management and maintenance services to its tenants. Offices would be opened in the Walton, Fairfield and Canning areas of Liverpool in addition to the Trust's registered offices in Bold Street where the Trust central services such as finance, computers, development, architectural and central management were provided from.

Much of LHT's work would continue for a very long period of time. Work in Canning

This page: *Before and after pictures of the renovation of Falkner Square, (top, both pictures) and Cathedral Mansions (above left and left).*

and its Cathedral Mansions would last for 20 years. The first properties were bought there in 1966 and the locality declared a general improvement area in 1969. LHT worked to restore the homes in the area, recreating original features, and completing all the work in 1986.

In Hebden Road, by the late 1970s, vandalism, poor construction and general deterioration of former MoD owned properties had led to serious deterioration. LHT replaced flat roofs with pitched ones and brought the properties up to a modern standard to create homes which occupants could be proud of.

Toxteth and Granby were of course devastated by rioting in 1981. Rebuilding homes and communities was a local and national priority once the dust had literally and metaphorically settled. LHT was instrumental in both new build and refurbishment in Princes Boulevard.

LHT's work would eventually extend all across Merseyside, for example taking over ownership of 2,800 homes from the Runcorn Development Corporation for the New Towns in 1987. Recognising that for a community to be successful there needs to be more than just housing, in 1998 LHT established an 'Extra Care' team to provide additional support for those in most need. Eight sheltered housing developments were provided and one housing with care

scheme aswell as 600 supported housing units. LHT also facilitates the May Logan healthy living centre which aims to help the local community take control of their health

and well-being and to improve the quality of their lives.

At the start of the new millennium LHT would have an annual income of £30 million, net assets of £95 million and was managing housing stock worth £262 million, an extraordinary achievement from such small beginnings.

Top right and above: *Princess Diana and HRH Princess Anne chat to residents after the opening of Florence Court (top) and Friendship House (above), 1989.*
Left and below: *Before and after the rehabilitated Hebden Road estate in Croxteth.*

Today LHT's head office is in Hanover Street and the Trust is moving towards a group structure to take full advantage of opportunities offered by market rent sector and housing stock transfer. The LHT Group will set future strategy and direction; LHT Housing will continue the traditional core activities in the social housing market; Cobalt Housing has been established to manage the stock transfer of 8,000 homes in the north of Liverpool; additionally Atrium City Living owns and manages a range of high quality homes to rent and for sale whilst also overseeing the work of LHT's student housing team which provides over 900 bed spaces.

Since the 1960s the streets of Liverpool have seen extraordinary changes. Many of us remember those days with affection, but few would us would want to return to the days of coal fires instead of central heating or exchange our indoor bathrooms for outside toilets.

Some communities were of course in worse condition than others. Liverpool 8 was then a tired worn out community with hundreds of sub standard homes. Few would want to live there today had things not changed. Fortunately the will, and determination of a few far sighted individuals energised the community; a process which would see sustained improvements being made not just for one year or even ten but down all the decades since the 1960s.

The community itself succeeded where local government failed, deciding that in the words once used by Royalty 'something must be done'. Many individuals contributed to the regeneration of the City both in small ways and large ways. But few contributed more than those who acted as midwives to the Liverpool Housing Trust, an organisation which, more than any other, would be responsible for turning areas round from being in terminal decline to ones in which residents can now feel proud to live.

Top: *Princes Boulevard after renovation, 1991.*
Above left and below: *The Granby Training Initiative Placement Scheme.*

Martindales - burning gold

The golden warmth of a brightly burning coal fire is one of the indelible memories of childhood for those of us over a certain age. For those us who were around before the advent of central heating, making the fire was a daily ritual for our mothers, and for youngsters the arrival of the coal man and his lorry are a memorable moment of excitement in our young lives.

For well over a century the Liverpool firm of Martindale's has been involved with managing energy related products and services. And throughout that long history the company has constantly evolved and developed to meet the changing needs of the market and its customers.

The business was founded in 1884 by Richard Lawson Martindale. Born in 1867 the young Richard Martindale had already had at least one major adventure in his life, having already joined in the Australian Gold Rush.

Richard however failed to strike it rich in Australia and returned to Liverpool empty handed. Undaunted, he sold his penny farthing bicycle to buy a cart and began to sell and deliver coal.

From premises in Crown Street, which would remain in use for ninety years, Martindale's - then still retaining its apostrophe - would in time become a major coal merchant with a family dynasty which would eventually include the founder's son, also Richard Lawson Martindale and in turn his son John Richard Lawson Martindale.

Above: Founder Richard Lawson Martindale and the Penny Farthing he sold to buy a cart.
Right: The offices occupied by Martindale's between 1937 and 1975. Below: A four wheel tipper outside the offices in 1971.

The second RL Martindale, born in 1919, would become a particularly well known local figure and following in the footsteps of his father became a chairman and director of Liverpool FC for 37 years.

It was in the years immediately following the end of first world war, however, which saw a rapid expansion of the business, one which would soon become the largest coal distributor in the North West.

In 1947, Richard Martindale's son John joined the company and oversaw further changes.

In the 1950s the business changed as coal began to be replaced by oil and gas. Martindale's entered the fuel oil market in the early 1950s and this in turn prompted a demand for the service and maintenance of oil-fired boilers. In the 1960s smokeless zones further reduced the demand for coal. Martindale's adapted to these changes by delivering other fuels and also developed installation, maintenance and conversion of heating boilers, from coal to oil or gas-fired, as an extension of its separate garage business which maintained the delivery vehicles for the fuel delivery fleet.

Diversification continued for some time. In the late 1950s the company took a controlling interest in Martindale and Carlyle, a motor dealership in Allerton Road, Liverpool, whilst the acquisition of the Manchester based company, Independent Gas Services, gave Martindale's a foothold in the gas servicing industry.

By the start of the 21st century the fourth generation of the Martindale family was represented by Managing Director Andrew Martindale and by Purchasing and Personnel Director Richard Martindale.

The Facilities Management division provides a comprehensive range of technical and non-technical services to clients' premises. This allows clients to focus on their core business, whilst Martindale's take responsibility for their office cleaning, postal services, building maintenance services and other client specific services.

Meanwhile Martindale's Fuel Services Division is one of the regions leading fuel distribution companies supplying a full range of petroleum products to the industrial, commercial, agricultural and retail sectors in Merseyside, Lancashire, Cheshire and Wales.

From one young man with a cart the business has grown to one employing 300 people; the head office is in Rose Place, St Anne Street to where it moved in 1974; there are also offices in North Wales, Runcorn, Manchester, Cardiff and Leeds.

In addition to Martindale's commitment to Health and Safety, they place a strong emphasis on staff training. The company runs an apprenticeship scheme in order to meet the projected growth of the business.

The company has embraced the IT 'revolution' and now uses the internet to communicate both with customers and its employees. Information about the company can now be viewed on its web site at www.martindales.co.uk

Young Richard Lawson Martindale may have failed to find gold in Australia but his Midas touch made sure that the Martindale family name still glitters in Liverpool.

The company now comprises six business divisions, which carry out the following services: Mechanical and Electrical Installation; Building Fit-Out and Refurbishment; Design, Manufacture and Installation of Building and Process Control Systems; Building Services Maintenance; Facilities Management; and Fuel Distribution.

Top left: A smart turn-out of drivers and vehicles pictured in Liverpool University's car park in 1982. Top right: One of Martindale's Building Services Maintenance representatives. Above left: Providing Site Facilities Management, thus allowing customers to totally focus on their business. Left and right: The company's Technical Services department providing expertise in building refurbishment (left) and the installation of mechanical and electrical equipment in the industrial, commercial and public sectors nationwide (right).

The Installation division installs mechanical and electrical equipment in the industrial, commercial and public sectors, nationwide. Based on 50 years experience in mechanical and electrical installation, the company provides full Project Management for the fit-out of new buildings and refurbishment of existing buildings, nationwide.

The Building Services Maintenance division employs some 200 multi-skilled service engineers who carry out mechanical and electrical installation on single and multi-site properties throughout the North of England and Wales.

Keep it clean

There are many things which form part of our lives which we spare little thought for. When we eat in a restaurant we never give the slightest thought to how the table cloth or napkins might be washed and ironed. And it's just the same at the places where we work: the only time we ever notice the towels in the wash rooms is if they are not there.

Mersey Towel Service was started in 1934 by William Arthur Hooker after he had been made redundant from the Naval Architects Department of the White Star Line; he began in business with the princely sum of £100.

The new company provided a towel hire service to the many offices and factories based in Liverpool. At first the firm was based at 4 Rumford Place in the city centre and employed just one delivery boy who used a bicycle to take the towels to offices around the city.

Though the company owned the towels it contracted out the actual washing to one of the many small independent laundries located in the city at that time - though tea towels and dusters were taken home to be washed by William's wife Jessica.

In those days office workers used hand towels whilst factory workers used Turkish roller towels (a continuous loop of towel hung on a wall-mounted bar) and 'Huckaback' hand and roller towels. Contact with factories soon led William to start offering to wash workers' overalls too.

William and Jessica's son, Norman Hooker, joined the company straight from school in 1942 and worked for his father until being called up. When Norman returned after his national service he rejoined the company and helped to build up the business. Bicycles would now become a thing of the past and the first delivery van in the, now traditional, dark red livery was bought soon after Norman's return.

Above: Founder William Arthur Hooker.
Below: A view inside the MTS production area circa 1970.

Things had to change some time, though two of the older washing machines had brass inner drums built to last and were still in use 40 years after their manufacture. Eventually however combined washer—extractors would come into use making washing and drying towels a much more efficient process.

But the business was by now not only supplying and washing towels. For example the contract washing and rental of table linen in many sizes and colours started in the 1960s.

Over the ensuing years the introduction of artificial fibres into the fabrics would bring even more colours, less shrinkage, better colour retention and easier processing.

Nor was table linen to be the end. More recently dust control mats of many sizes and colours along with Logo mats used to promote corporate identity and image have been introduced.

Norman Hooker died in 1996 after having semi-retired; Giles Hooker the third generation of his family to run the company joined it in 1986.

The area now covered by the business extends out from Merseyside to South Lancashire, St Helens, Runcorn and the Wirral - the firm has certainly come a long way from the time when it could operate with one man and a boy with a bike!

Business increased steadily and in 1954 it was decided it was more economic to wash the towels in-house than to contract out. A separate laundry company was soon started, the Mersey Towel Service (Laundry) Ltd based at 16/18 Whiteford Street L6, although at this time an office was still maintained at Rumford Place. The business however continued to expand until the laundry in Whiteford Street reached full capacity. A decision was made to move to even larger premises, and on 9th August 1961 MTS (Laundry) Ltd bought the long-established Birchfield Laundry at 1-3 Birchfield Road L7 in the Stoneycroft area of the city - premises where MTS is still based. As a result of acquiring the Birchfield Road laundry MTS now left both Rumford Place and Whiteford Street.

Times were changing. During the 1960s the now familiar Cabinet Roller Towel was introduced, an item of washroom furniture which is still a major sector in the industry. Meanwhile back at the laundry technology was moving on too: the firm had previously used washing machines and then had to transfer items into 'hydros' or spin - dryers to the man or woman in the street.

Top left: The Wash House, 1970s.
Above left: Mr Norman Hooker.
Below left: Giles Hooker, current Managing Director.
Bottom: The company's Birchfield Road premises in the 1970s.

Changing the face of Liverpool

Wrenco. Does the name ring a bell? It should do, the firm has been involved in innumerable civil engineering projects around Liverpool since 1964.

The founders of Wrenco (Contractors) Ltd - Terry Bolland, Jimmy McMahon, Tom McGuire and Emlyn 'Em' Roberts first met through a common involvement with a self-build housing group. In such schemes the members, whether tradesmen, professionals or labourers teamed up on an equal basis to provide a home for each member through their collective toil.

The notion occurred to Terry and Jimmy that the same ethos might be successfully applied to a business venture and they in turn put their idea to Tom and Emlyn who readily joined up. Thus the 'gang of four' pooled the talents of two foremen, an accountant/business adviser and a quantity surveyor. All they were short of was work.

The very first job was a Labour-Only Contract to excavate, by hand the foundations of an office development at Widnes. Some of the stanchion bases were more than twenty feet deep but Jimmy and Tom tore into it with such verve and vigour that it convinced the site agent that he need look no further for resources for the remainder of the contract - nor did the agent baulk when Emlyn arrived each Friday to 'agree the measure' and ensure that every inch of work and every drop of sweat was paid for at premium rates. Extra labour was recruited and the contract went on for some six months, at the end of which there was a very handy lump of working capital in the bank.

To protect the fragile finances of the fledgling firm an arrangement was struck that although the on-site people would work full-time for a basic salary the two professional types would keep their existing occupations and take only a fraction of the same salary, integrating only as the firm grew. It would be 1968 before all four were fully committed on an equal basis, each one both learning from and working for the others.

Meanwhile, the momentum was maintained with cable-laying contracts from the G.P.O. and domestic garage building for the surrounding local authorities. As the sixties drew to a close the company had earned sufficient respect from local authorities to be awarded major road contracts such as duelling of the A41 New Chester Road at Bebington and also of Borough Road, Birkenhead followed by the re-vamping of the Mersey Tunnel approaches at Birkenhead. There were also two major sewerage schemes at Hoylake and Banks which were

Right: Ben Peters who in 1970 at the age of 65 joined the firm as clerical assistant.
Below left: The 1982 Garden Festival site.
Below: Liverpool Anglican Cathedral Precinct Plaza where over £1 million pounds worth of construction work was carried out by Wrenco.

acquired a site and built its present premises on the industrial estate at Sefton Lane, Maghull.

The 1970s brought work from the Development Corporations at Runcorn, Warrington, Skelmersdale and Central Lancs. The company began recruiting local school leavers, two of whom, Dave Brooks and Mike Williams, would eventually hold key positions in Wrenco.

The Merseyside Development Corporation, set up in the 1980s to change the face of Liverpool, provided many contracts for Wrenco during its fourteen year regeneration process from the initial Garden Festival Project through to the construction of the Leeds St/Old Hall St/Gt Howard St junction in 1996. The 1990s brought a rash of town centre refurbishments in Liverpool, Kirby, Manchester, Leigh, Tyldsley and Widnes for Wrenco whilst in 2000 the company completed the £3 million refurbishment of the Princes Dock Basin at the Pier Head.

Today, though remaining a medium sized firm, Wrenco is one with strong capabilities - and it remains just as ready for a challenge at the start of the third Millennium as it was on the day it was conceived by those four idealistic young men back in 1964.

won and duly completed within budget and on time. Another scheme at Ormskirk provided special interest for Wrenco. The council received letters from the local residents praising both the courtesy of the men, and the progress of their work. In recognition of this the Chairman, in his official car, decided to make a surprise visit to the site to drink a Champagne toast to Jimmy McMahon and his drainage team! It was fortunate for Wrenco that the story, with pictures, was picked up by the national daily papers which provided welcome publicity.

By now people had been recruited, who, with the founders, would become the bedrock of the company: Don Lucas, Chief Q.S. and Contracts Manager, who would lead the operations in the 1980s and 90s; Rick Hudson (Engineer), John Coady, Tommy Brennan, Ted Wickham, Martin McGuire and the late Mick Flanagan (all Foremen) and good old Ben Peters, clerical assistant extraordinaire who in 1970, at the age of 65, asked if he could join the company for one day as a trial and never missed a single day, six days a week, until he passed away in 1987. Also at that time the company

*Top left: Refurbishment of the Princes Dock. **Top right:** The impressive new entrance to Kirby town centre. **Left:** Still going strong, with a combined total of one hundred and twenty-seven years service at Wrenco; (left to right) Bert Savage (twenty-five years), John Coady (thirty-four years), Wally Burns (thirty-five years) and Ted Wickham (thirty-three years).*

Wood you believe it?

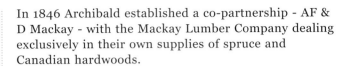

The privately owned Liverpool timber-trading firm of AF & D Mackay has been in the business now for more than one and a half centuries.

The Mackay family had travelled from Scotland to Canada's Nova Scotia in 1760 and found prosperity there. In the 1820s the Mackay Lumber Company was established in St John, New Brunswick trading extensively in Canada and overseas. Remarkably the company did not own a single sawmill; its entrepreneurial skill lay in advancing money to small growers and mill operators in exchange for a percentage of their production.

In 1843 Archibald Fraser Mackay arrived in Liverpool to oversee that end of the family export business; he set up an agency opposite Queen's Dock. At that time the timber trade was based at the Brunswick Dock, the southern extremity of the docks system, where scores of sailing vessels moored to discharge their cargoes.

In 1846 Archibald established a co-partnership - AF & D Mackay - with the Mackay Lumber Company dealing exclusively in their own supplies of spruce and Canadian hardwoods.

The firm prospered during the second half of the 19th century and by the 1900s was shipping over 100,000 'standards' annually.

With the decline of sail the timber trade migrated to the north end of the port and the firm set up offices and yards at 10 Old Canada Dock where it remained until work started on the present day Canada Dock: 'Mackays' then moved to the most prestigious address in Liverpool the Royal Liver Building in the early 20th century.

The Canadian side of the business was run by W Malcolm Mackay from 1875 to 1915 when he was succeeded by his son Hugh. It was Hugh who led the firm through the prosperity brought about by the first world war and the dark days of the 1920s. He remained until 1930 when he diversified into other commercial ventures and entered the world of politics; at the time of his death in 1957 he was leader of the New Brunswick Conservative Party.

Above: Company founders AF Mackay (left) and D Mackay (right). **Right:** *Logs being floated downriver to the timber yards in Nova Scotia.* **Below:** *Transporting the cut logs to the river.*

were quickly up and running in those countries. It was a testament to Bill Boulton that these two sources would account for a high proportion of the company's 200,000 sq. mtrs annual sales.

In June 1924 the firm became a limited company when it was by far the largest shipper of Canadian Spruce to the UK.

The last of the New Brunswick timbermen, Charles Mackay, died in 1975 after many years of service in Liverpool, and with him ended almost 130 years of his family's involvement in the UK timber trade.

In 1936 an attempt by the Inland Revenue to levy taxes on the St John office on the profits of the Liverpool office led to the division of the joint company. The Canadian operation came under the control of Colin Mackay who bought out those members of his family whose interests lay in politics and academia. The death of Colin in 1964 saw the last of the involvement of the Mackays in New Brunswick and led to the take-over of that company by JD Irving Ltd of St John who would continue to be important suppliers.

In 1988 after a brief period of external ownership the company was bought back by Martin and Bill Boulton who became Managing Director and Chairman respectively. Since that date the company has continued to grow and prosper with the balance of trade shifting even more so from Canada to Scandinavia where their connections in Sweden and Norway remain particularly strong today.

An illustrious history is no guarantee of future prosperity; during the mid 1960s the management in Liverpool realised that they should not rely on Canadian sources alone.

The timber industry has changed continually throughout the long years of AF & D Mackay's history; but though the company's roots may be firmly planted in the past its sights are solidly focused on adapting to the future.

William H Boulton joined the company in 1962 and had been made a director in 1966; he would later be Managing Director and eventually Chairman.

*Top left: The Frederiction Hardwood Mill, 1937. **Top right:** The Trans-Canada Highway running through one of the timber yards. **Above:** A Forbes Mackay. **Below:** Gloucester Spruce being loaded for export.*

It was Bill Boulton who took responsibility for diversifying into Scandinavia and he set about establishing the kind of long term personal relationships which had served the company so well in the past. With assistance from such friends as Erling Lyche in Norway and Roland Sydell, Bjorn Erlandsson and Gunnar Weltergren in Sweden Mackays

On the tiles

Ceramic tiles have changed incredibly over what seems like a very short period of time. These days if you look in the nation's kitchens and bathrooms there seems to be an incredible variety of tiles in use: plain and patterned, a whole rainbow of colours and an infinite variety of shapes and textures.

It wasn't always like that of course. Many readers' recollection of tiles in the home will be limited to those around the fireplace; the only places they were likely to see large areas of tiles were in public buildings such as hospitals and museums where they tended to be of rather sober and uninspiring shades of brown and green.

But not so today. Inspired by endless television home improvement programmes our homes are now almost invariably beautified by the addition of high quality ceramic tiles. And in Liverpool there is a good chance we bought them from Everton Glass Works.

In 1947, at the age of 41, Stanley Charles Richards a former glazier started the firm from premises at 19A Heyworth Street. From there he supplied glass, glazing and decorating products to the public and the trade. Eventually he would acquire two more shops in the area from where he would trade successfully for many years.

In the mid 1960s, when Heyworth Street was being demolished, and while one side of the road was being pulled down, the firm acquired two shops on the opposite side, on the corner of Eastlake Street and Stansfield Road.

By this time his eldest son Alan had joined him and ran the decorating side of the business, and soon after his youngest son Stanley Jnr came into the business and eventually worked in the glass, doors, and ceramic tiles section.

That was far from being the last move however. The whole business was moved to 54-56 Townsend Lane around 1969 from where it continued to trade in exactly the same products.

Top left: *Founder of the company Stanley Charles Richards.*
Below: *The Everton Glassworks 1960s premises on the corner of Eastlake Street and Heyworth Street.*

In 1972 the premises at 54-56 Townsend Lane were sold to Panorama Kitchens and Everton Glassworks bought 60-64 Townsend Lane two doors further along.

Around 1981, when Pat Lewis, the founder's daughter started working for the company, the firm bought 46-50 Townsend Lane and moved its glass and doors business there and later began selling ceramic tiles there too, leaving 60-64 for the decorating side of the business.

Stanley Richards died in 1983 and his firm then passed to the next generation.

Refurbishment was the order of the day in 1986 when 46-50 Townsend Lane was extensively altered and the tile side of the business, which by then was doing very well, was expanded.

Indeed, because of increased business in ceramic tiles in 1991, the family acquired a 10,000 sq ft warehouse at 19a Belmont Road (clearly a lucky number, the second time it had turned up.)

But even that was not enough. In 1997, after being unable to extend the warehouse in Belmont Road and unable to get another property with a suitable warehouse in Liverpool, the firm now took the lease on a 6,000 sq ft warehouse in Bolton in order to cope with the expansion of the ceramic tile side of the business.

Alan has since retired and his daughter Shirley now manages the wallpaper and decorating business. Stanley's son Jonathan has also joined the company and manages the tile and door business.

By 2001 the businesses in both Liverpool and Bolton were each subject to major refurbishment. This gave even more opportunities for customers to see all the stock that was available in Everton Glass Works new showrooms where the family continues in its business of selling its goods at very competitive prices in a friendly but efficient way.

Stanley Richards would have been astonished to see just how far the small business he established in Heyworth Street back in 1947 had managed to progress in a little over fifty years. He would probably be even more surprised to know just how obsessed the British have become with home improvements over that period. Thank goodness firms like Everton Glass Works exist in order to meet our apparently limitless appetites for such products. And thank goodness too that we have a wider choice of tiles today than the limited selection of utility white, institution brown and hospital green which were all that seemed to be on offer in the days of long ago.

Above: The firms former shop on the corner of Stansfield Road and Heyworth Street. *Below:* The company Head Office in Townsend Lane.

Books fit for a Queen

Books, don't we all love them? But the written word was once valued far more highly than it is today, and fine leather bindings and gold leaf were commonplace in books, reflecting the respect accorded to them.

Thomas Loughlin Ltd was founded in 1891 to specialise in machine-ruling and hand-craft bookbinding. The business began from premises in School Lane, an area then full of printers and book-binders. Three staff were employed: a 'machine ruler', a lady make-up and book sewer and a bookbinder and gold finisher.

Paper was still bought by the pound rather than priced in grams per square metre and cost a guinea (£1.05) a ream, whilst leather skins bought from Glasgow tanneries were two guineas each. Pure gold too was used - unlike today when gold foil is used - burnished on using hot branding tools heated on a gas-ring.

Those were the days when many shopkeepers counted on their fingers and account books in £sd (pounds shillings and pence) were still the order of the day. Until the late 1980s this three generation family company would still offer machine ruling and large ledgers for all those businesses which were slow to install computer technology.

Paper was in very short supply during the world wars, but the firm survived. In the first world war the firm temporarily lost the services of its very young machine-ruler Bill Davies. He returned to continue working for the company, but astonishingly he joined the forces for a second time in 1940!

During the second world war School Lane was blitzed and the firm moved to Whitefield Road before eventually moving on to modern premises in Canning Place.

Right: *Binder applying gold leaf with branding roll.* **Below:** *Opening spread of 'Queens Commemorative Visit to Liverpool' copies of which can be found in Buckingham Palace and the Liverpool Town Hall.*

By now the founder, Old Tommy Loughlin, had long been joined by his son 'Young' Tommy. Young Tommy's son, Ken, would later join the family firm too.

Business was more leisurely in those days, however, than today. The boss Thomas Loughlin would always arrive at 9am, get his cup of tea and stop the machine-ruler 'Old Bill' Davies and the apprentice and talk football for at least an hour - not least about his own youthful experiences playing for Blyth Spartans as a semipro, before reminding the pair that he had supplied the paper for Manchester United's first ever programme which they had sold themselves at Wembley.

Thomas Loughlin Ltd was always chosen and commissioned to provide crafted leather bound books on state occasions such as the opening of both Mersey Tunnels, the Queen's commemorative visit to Liverpool and the opening of the National Garden Festival, and the Tall Ships Race.

On each occasion Her Majesty was presented with a large gilded volume for her archives at Buckingham Palace and the Liverpool City Council with a copy for the Town Hall library. On a more sombre note the company also provided the memorial book for the families who lost relatives in the sinking of the MV Derbyshire.

At the instigation of Ken Loughlin the company's first folding-machine had been bought around 1968 and transformed the make up of the business, improving production to such a degree that since then the company, now led by its current Managing Director, Mr Tony Aspey, has invested and re-invested in more and more new equipment to such an extent that it would become the North West's leading print finisher. Folding progressed to perfect binding, then to sewn and casebinding with miniature and wire binding as further additions.

Today the company's purpose-built factory near the motorway network, the Glacier Building in Harrington Road, contains the very latest in PC technology and features state of the art equipment controlled by dedicated staff who are totally proficient at their craft.

Surprisingly Thomas Loughlin Ltd's reputation for quality has been spread by word of mouth. The firm has never had a representative on the road. That enviable reputation has seen the firm's annual turnover rise from less than £1,000 a year to over £3 million.

From humble beginnings, far back in the reign of Queen Victoria, Thomas Loughlin Ltd has come a very long way indeed. But despite the distance it has travelled in terms of business success it has fortunately still managed to retain the values which its founder would have approved of - not least an unsurpassed dedication to quality.

Above left: *Gold foil blocking.*
Top right *The finished product.*
Left: *The new print finishing factory floor.*

Pat pending

Build a better mousetrap and the world will beat a path to your door. That old saying is undoubtedly true to a point; but if the mousetrap builder doesn't patent his invention then DIY enthusiasts all over the world will be busy beating a path to their own garden sheds to knock up their own versions of the novel rodent killer.

Yes it's all very well having a brilliant idea but unless that idea is patented someone else will inevitably steal, borrow or copy it without paying the inventor a penny.

Applying for a patent, and if one is lucky, later exploiting its potential by licensing is a tricky thing to do; and it's not something which horny handed inventors are likely to have much experience of. Wise inventors stick to what they know and hand over that part of the job to a patent agent.

Patent agents have been around for as long as it has been possible to register a patent and gain the grant of a temporary monopoly on one's new idea. In the north west of

England, a place full of fertile and inventive minds, there has never been a shortage of people with bright ideas.

One of Liverpool's best known patent agents are the firm Roystons. The business was founded in 1865 by Frederick J Cheesbrough a consulting engineer and patent agent of 43 Castle Street on the corner of Harrington Street, Liverpool.

In 1878 the founder was joined by Ernest Richard Royston and the pair traded as Cheesbrough and Royston moving to Canton Buildings 15, Water Street in 1892. Frederick Cheesbrough left the firm in the early 1900s and the business moved to Tower Buildings in Water Street.

Above: The Principal ER Royston in private office.
Right: Canton Buildings, Roystons first offices.
Below: Tower Buildings from where Roystons have traded for over a century.

especially in the USA. Roystons handles all kinds of intellectual property issues: handling the filing of patents, designs and trademark applications and advises on infringement matters, licensing and related matters. The firm will help clients secure legal rights for their new products, ideas and brands which will help them obtain market leads and shares or earn money from licensing or selling those rights.

Roystons has seen the 19th century, the 20th century and now the start of the 21st. At the outset the work was very labour intensive requiring copywriter and draftsmen; today fewer staff are required with the arrival of computers. But though old skills may go, new ones are required. Staff with different technical backgrounds are needed as biotechnology and computer related inventions replace the older engineering type patent applications. Nor does the law remain static; those who seek to protect their patents and trademarks must now grapple with the introduction of a European patent system, the Patent Co-operation Treaty and the Community Trademark system.

The firm remains there to this day, although having moved up from the 3rd to the 6th floor, via a period on the 4th floor, during the intervening years.

In the late 1920s JE Lloyd Barnes joined the firm; a well known figure he had been a President of the Chartered Institute of Patent Agents in 1924. By now the firm had become known as ER Royston & Co., a name which would remain unaltered until 1977.

In the decades following JE Lloyd Barnes' arrival various other names joined the firm, individuals such as David MacMillan Haig and John Shevlin Wilson. In the 1970s another Liverpool firm, AC Ashton & Co. of Refuge House, 12 Lord Street, merged with Royston & Co.

And Ashton & Co was not the only merger. An assistant at ER Royston & Co., John Hindley Walker, had left to set up his own business in around 1906, specialising in patent work and his daughter in trademarks. In the 1970s this firm too merged with ER Royston & Co. and the new firm took the simpler name Roystons.

Today Roystons has a large client base extending throughout England and Wales; the firm also has many foreign clients

Yes, these changes may present problems, but the history of Roystons is one of solving problems not succumbing to them - for well over a century those with a better mousetrap have been beating a path to Roystons door to ensure that the world will, in turn, beat a path to theirs.

*Top left: Intermediate general office, leading to typing offices. **Centre:** A guide to patents and inventions by ER Royston, 1902. **Right:** Intermediate general office.*

The ultimate service

According to the old adage there are only two certainties in life - death and taxes. The very rich and the very poor may avoid taxes, but none of us avoid death. And if the manner of our passing may matter little to us once we are gone it is very important to the bereaved.

They want not only to see us end our days with dignity but also to see that their final farewells are made with fitting decorum. Until the 19th century however few funerals for ordinary folk left their mark. Our great churches and cathedrals were, and still are, filled with the effigies of, and memorials to, the great and the good, but most ordinary people had to be content with much less. For the average man or woman laying out would be conducted by a local woman who was probably a neighbour who did this on part time basis - and often doubled up as a midwife. The local carpenter would make a coffin and the burial in the local church-yard would, like as not, be marked with a simple wooden cross which would disappear in a few years time.

The demand for elaborate funerals reached its height in the Victorian era as witnessed by the many elaborate memorials in Liverpool's graveyards. And with that funerary elaboration rose the profession of modern undertaker.

But not all firms of funeral directors were founded quite as long ago as the Victorian age.

Walter Craven began arranging funerals in the early 1920s from premises at 2 Broadgreen Road, Old Swan, Liverpool where he employed just two staff - today the firm has 65 employees.

Above left: Desmond Craven, son of the founder.
Below: The funeral of Archbishop Downey in 1953, furnished by Leadbetter & Murphy.

Though brought up in St Helens Walter had moved to Liverpool after the Great War. Before starting his undertaking service Walter had been involved in long distance Rolls Royce hire, meeting ships from America at Liverpool and taking passengers on to Newcastle to catch connecting vessels to Scandinavia or south to London. Walter also provided a luxury taxi service for Liverpool's upper classes.

Luxury taxi and wedding car work would continue in tandem with the funeral services business for many years, though with the funeral side of the business taking up an ever greater proportion of time.

A branch at Page Moss was opened in 1938 on the eve of the second world war. In anticipation of massive civilian casualties the government made being a funeral director a reserved occupation during World War II. As a result, the founder's son, Desmond, who had now joined his father, was not called up but instead served as member of the Auxiliary Fire Service during hostilities.

The early 1950s saw the acquisition of Craven Lodge in Broadgreen Road which was then an elegant, though very old, house. That old building was replaced by the company's modern, purpose built premises in 1970.

Times were changing. It was in the 1970s that solid oak and elm coffins would begin to be replaced, first by mahogany, and then by today's familiar veneered chipboard - though there is still the occasional client who requires a sold oak coffin or an American style casket.

The present chairman, Derek Craven, grandson of the founder, joined the firm in 1963. Since then other local businesses have been acquired: Moar & Butler of Widnes in 1964, Charlett's in South Liverpool in 1968, Maddock's in Warrington in 1979 and Leadbetter & Murphy in 1984. In addition a new funeral home was opened in Lugsmore Lane, St Helens in 1989.

Today the fourth generation of the Craven family, Charles Craven, great grandson of the founder is Managing Director. He continues the fine traditions handed down through his family since the 1920s: constant care, and attention to the smallest detail at a time in people's lives when even small errors, normally insignificant, assume vast importance. And in these days of ever larger firms it is a refreshing change for the bereaved to still be able to speak directly to the man in charge.

Above: *A Craven & Company invoice from 1953.*
Above left: *Craven Lodge foyer.*
Left: *Walter Craven's impressive fleet of limousines.*

Forming an orderly queue for Wilkie's Circus in New Brighton in the 1940s.

Acknowledgments

The publishers would like to thank

Liverpool Libraries and Information Services

Reflections - Black & White Photographic Archive - www.20thcenturyimages.co.uk

John Thornton

Andrew Mitchell

Steve Ainsworth

True North Books Ltd - Book List

Memories of Accrington - 1 903204 05 4

Memories of Barnet - 1 903204 16 X

Memories of Barnsley - 1 900463 11 3

Golden Years of Barnsley -1 900463 87 3

Memories of Basingstoke - 1 903204 26 7

Memories of Bedford - 1 900463 83 0

More Memories of Bedford - 1 903204 33 X

Golden Years of Birmingham - 1 900463 04 0

Birmingham Memories - 1 903204 45 3

Memories of Blackburn - 1 900463 40 7

More Memories of Blackburn - 1 900463 96 2

Memories of Blackpool - 1 900463 21 0

Memories of Bolton - 1 900463 45 8

More Memories of Bolton - 1 900463 13 X

Bolton Memories - 1 903204 37 2

Memories of Bournemouth -1 900463 44 X

Memories of Bradford - 1 900463 00 8

More Memories of Bradford - 1 900463 16 4

More Memories of Bradford II - 1 900463 63 6

Bradford Memories - 1 903204 47 X

Bradford City Memories - 1 900463 57 1

Memories of Bristol - 1 900463 78 4

More Memories of Bristol - 1 903204 43 7

Memories of Bromley - 1 903204 21 6

Memories of Burnley - 1 900463 95 4

Golden Years of Burnley - 1 900463 67 9

Memories of Bury - 1 900463 90 3

Memories of Cambridge - 1 900463 88 1

Memories of Cardiff - 1 900463 14 8

Memories of Carlisle - 1 900463 38 5

Memories of Chelmsford - 1 903204 29 1

Memories of Cheltenham - 1 903204 17 8

Memories of Chester - 1 900463 46 6

More Memories of Chester -1 903204 02 X

Memories of Chesterfield -1 900463 61 X

More Memories of Chesterfield - 1 903204 28 3

Memories of Colchester - 1 900463 74 1

Nostalgic Coventry - 1 900463 58 X

Coventry Memories - 1 903204 38 0

Memories of Croydon - 1 900463 19 9

More Memories of Croydon - 1 903204 35 6

Golden Years of Darlington - 1 900463 72 5

Nostalgic Darlington - 1 900463 31 8

Darlington Memories - 1 903204 46 1

Memories of Derby - 1 900463 37 7

More Memories of Derby - 1 903204 20 8

Memories of Dewsbury & Batley - 1 900463 80 6

Memories of Doncaster - 1 900463 36 9

Nostalgic Dudley - 1 900463 03 2

Memories of Edinburgh - 1 900463 33 4

Memories of Enfield - 1 903204 14 3

Memories of Exeter - 1 900463 94 6

Memories of Glasgow - 1 900463 68 7

More Memories of Glasgow - 1 903204 44 5

Memories of Gloucester - 1 903204 04 6

Memories of Grimsby - 1 900463 97 0

More Memories of Grimsby - 1 903204 36 4

Memories of Guildford - 1 903204 22 4

Memories of Halifax - 1 900463 05 9

More Memories of Halifax - 1 900463 06 7

Golden Years of Halifax - 1 900463 62 8

Nostalgic Halifax - 1 903204 30 5

Memories of Harrogate - 1 903204 01 1

Memories of Hartlepool - 1 900463 42 3

Memories of High Wycombe - 1 900463 84 9

Memories of Huddersfield - 1 900463 15 6

More Memories of Huddersfield - 1 900463 26 1

Golden Years of Huddersfield - 1 900463 77 6

Nostalgic Huddersfield - 1 903204 19 4

Huddersfield Town FC - 1 900463 51 2

Memories of Hull - 1 900463 86 5

More Memories of Hull - 1 903204 06 2

Memories of Ipswich - 1 900463 09 1

More Memories of Ipswich - 1 903204 52 6

Memories of Keighley - 1 900463 01 6

Golden Years of Keighley - 1 900463 92 X

Memories of Kingston - 1 903204 24 0

Memories of Leeds - 1 900463 75 X

Continued overleaf

True North Books Ltd - Book List

More Memories of Leeds - 1 900463 12 1

Golden Years of Leeds - 1 903204 07 0

Memories of Leicester - 1 900463 08 3

More Memories of Leicester - 1 903204 08 9

Memories of Leigh - 1 903204 27 5

Memories of Lincoln - 1 900463 43 1

Memories of Liverpool - 1 900463 07 5

More Memories of Liverpool - 1 903204 09 7

Liverpool Memories - 1 903204 53 4

Memories of Luton - 1 900463 93 8

Memories of Macclesfield - 1 900463 28 8

Memories of Manchester - 1 900463 27 X

More Memories of Manchester - 1 903204 03 8

Manchester Memories - 1 903204 54 2

Memories of Middlesbrough - 1 900463 56 3

More Memories of Middlesbrough - 1 903204 42 9

Memories of Newbury - 1 900463 79 2

Memories of Newcastle - 1 900463 81 4

More Memories of Newcastle - 1 903204 10 0

Memories of Newport - 1 900463 59 8

Memories of Northampton - 1 900463 48 2

More Memories of Northampton - 1 903204 34 8

Memories of Norwich - 1 900463 73 3

Memories of Nottingham - 1 900463 91 1

More Memories of Nottingham - 1 903204 11 9

Bygone Oldham - 1 900463 25 3

Memories of Oldham - 1 900463 76 8

Memories of Oxford - 1 900463 54 7

Memories of Peterborough - 1 900463 98 9

Golden Years of Poole - 1 900463 69 5

Memories of Portsmouth - 1 900463 39 3

More Memories of Portsmouth - 1 903204 51 8

Nostalgic Preston - 1 900463 50 4

More Memories of Preston - 1 900463 17 2

Preston Memories - 1 903204 41 0

Memories of Reading - 1 900463 49 0

Memories of Rochdale - 1 900463 60 1

More Memories of Reading - 1 903204 39 9

More Memories of Rochdale - 1 900463 22 9

Memories of Romford - 1 903204 40 2

Memories of St Albans - 1 903204 23 2

Memories of St Helens - 1 900463 52 0

Memories of Sheffield - 1 900463 20 2

More Memories of Sheffield - 1 900463 32 6

Golden Years of Sheffield - 1 903204 13 5

Memories of Slough - 1 900 463 29 6

Golden Years of Solihull - 1 903204 55 0

Memories of Southampton - 1 900463 34 2

More Memories of Southampton - 1 903204 49 6

Memories of Stockport - 1 900463 55 5

More Memories of Stockport - 1 903204 18 6

Memories of Stockton - 1 900463 41 5

Memories of Stoke-on-Trent - 1 900463 47 4

More Memories of Stoke-on-Trent - 1 903204 12 7

Memories of Stourbridge - 1903204 31 3

Memories of Sunderland - 1 900463 71 7

More Memories of Sunderland - 1 903204 48 8

Memories of Swindon - 1 903204 00 3

Memories of Uxbridge - 1 900463 64 4

Memories of Wakefield - 1 900463 65 2

More Memories of Wakefield - 1 900463 89 X

Nostalgic Walsall - 1 900463 18 0

Golden Years of Walsall - 1 903204 56 9

More Memories of Warrington - 1 900463 02 4

Memories of Watford - 1 900463 24 5

Golden Years of West Bromwich - 1 900463 99 7

Memories of Wigan - 1 900463 85 7

Golden Years of Wigan - 1 900463 82 2

Nostalgic Wirral - 1 903204 15 1

Memories of Woking - 1 903204 32 1

Nostalgic Wolverhampton - 1 900463 53 9

Wolverhampton Memories - 1 903204 50 X

Memories of Worcester - 1 903204 25 9

Memories of Wrexham - 1 900463 23 7

Memories of York - 1 900463 66 0